Dr David Harrison is a UK based Masonic historian who has so far written ten books on the history of English Freemasonry and has contributed many papers and articles on the subject to various journals and magazines, such as the *AQC*, *Philalethes Journal*, the UK based *Freemasonry Today*, *MQ Magazine*, *The Square*, the US based *Knight Templar Magazine* and the *Masonic Journal*. Harrison has also appeared frequently on TV and radio discussing his work. Having gained his PhD from the University of Liverpool in 2008, which focused on the development of English Freemasonry, the thesis was subsequently published in March 2009 entitled *The Genesis of Freemasonry* by Lewis Masonic. The work became a best seller and is now on its third edition. Harrison's other works include *The Transformation of Freemasonry* published by Arima Publishing in 2010, the *Liverpool Masonic Rebellion and the Wigan Grand Lodge* also published by Arima in 2012, *A Quick Guide to Freemasonry* which was published by Lewis Masonic in 2013, an examination of the *York Grand Lodge* published in 2014, *Freemasonry and Fraternal Societies* published in 2015, *The City of York: A Masonic Guide* published in 2016, and a biography on 19th century Liverpool philanthropist *Christopher Rawdon* which was published in the same year. His work *The Lost Rites and Rituals of Freemasonry* was published by Lewis Masonic in 2017, and Harrison's next work *Rediscovered Rituals of English Freemasonry* is due out in May 2020. Harrison regularly gives lectures on many aspects of Masonic history to lodges and conferences all over the world and is a Past Master of the Lodge of Lights No. 148 in the West Lancashire Province under the United Grand Lodge of England. He is also a Fellow of the Philalethes and a member of numerous side-orders.

Dedicated to my muse

A Journey Through Freemasonry

David Harrison

Published 2019 by arima publishing

www.arimapublishing.com

ISBN 978 1 84549 760 6

© David Harrison 2019

Typeset in Garamond

arima publishing
ASK House, Northgate Avenue
Bury St Edmunds, Suffolk IP32 6BB
t: (+44) 01284 700321
www.arimapublishing.com

Foreword

In this wonderful and edifying Masonic anecdote, the brilliant Dr David Harrison entertains us while he instructs us with his historical brushstrokes about Freemasonry that transport us to a past world forged by Freemasonry. Freemasonry seems to have been involved in many more things than we might give credit to today and Harrison provides us with a broad and rich context in his Masonic Mosaic, from the conflicts between Ancient and Modern to Freemasonry during the French Revolution through incredible Titans of Freemasonry and the history and intra-history of humanity: Thomas Paine the reformer and progressivist; Edward Jenner the creator of the smallpox vaccine; Sir Thomas Raffles founder of Singapore and firm abolitionist of slavery; writers Jerome K Jerome, Conan Doyle and Thomas de Quincey the famous opium eater; the incredible story of Joseph Brant ... Harrison writes in an accessible way and does not overload the reader with facts and dates, rather implants in him the seeds of wanting to know more about the topics outlined in this great book that I hope Mason readers and Non freemasons alike will enjoy.

Darren Lorente-Bull, Masonic author, London. December 2019.

A Journey through Freemasonry

Ever since I began to research my PhD thesis on the origins and development of English Freemasonry at the University of Liverpool in 2000, I started to write articles for Masonic magazines in the UK and US such as *MQ*, *Freemasonry Today*, *The Ashlar*, *Philalethes*, *Knight Templar Magazine*, and *The Square*, amongst others. These were all highly regarded and excellent magazines in their own right, all dealing with the history, philosophy and current news of Freemasonry, most having an international readership.

I have thus written around a hundred articles over the past twenty years, and when it was put to me to compile my favourite articles in a *Compendium*, it gave me the opportunity to not only choose my favourite pieces, but also the articles that I received the most positive feedback from by the readers. Various different magazines have their own in-house style; some magazines wanted footnotes for example, others did not, some wanted photos, others supplied their own. It also gave me an insight into editing and publishing, and also gave me an opportunity to meet other well-known writers and editors such as Michael Baigent.

Coming from an academic background, and being a lecturer of local history, much of my subject matter was drawn from that interest, such as the *Liverpool Masonic Rebellion* and my work on the *York Grand Lodge*, both subjects becoming articles in various magazines and being the basis for future books. Other articles where particularly requested, such as *Freemasonry and the French Revolution* which is also featured in this book. Some articles reflected my interest and research such as my work concerning Thomas Paine and Joseph Brant, while other articles reflected my interest in archaeology, such as the tunnels of Joseph Williamson, the Hell Fire caves of Sir Francis Dashwood and the now derelict Woolton Hall in Liverpool. All however, reflected Masonic themes.

As an academic, I also conducted research and wrote papers on the topic of Freemasonry that appeared in many academic journals, and I have also included some of those papers in this book. Some of my papers found homes in renowned Masonic journals such as *Heredom*, *AQC* and *The Journal for Research into Freemasonry and Fraternalism*, and were presented at various conferences and at universities. Most of the articles presented in this collection have a related theme; that of Freemasons changing the world for the force of good, be it natural philosophers that have made an advancement in medicine such as Edward Jenner, men of science and revolutionary politics such as Benjamin Franklin and men that took a strong stance against the slave trade such as Thomas Stamford Raffles. My aim with this book is not only to collect the most popular articles and papers together in one source, but to allow Masons and indeed non-Masons, to present the articles themselves.

Dr David Harrison,
Historian and Master Mason

Contents

Part 1: Masonic Personalities

Edward Jenner – Freemason

Edward Jenner is one of my all-time favourite Freemasons, mainly because his work on the smallpox vaccine saved countless millions of lives. I was also attracted to the Enlightenment era of the eighteenth century and how Freemasonry entwined itself with this ethos. This article appeared in *Freemasonry Today* in autumn 2010.

It has been said that the discovery of the smallpox vaccine in the late eighteenth century by Freemason, Edward Jenner has saved more lives than the work of any other man: Jenner has been fairly described as the 'father of immunology'. The publication in 1798 of Jenner's findings that cowpox could protect against the feared and usually fatal disease – smallpox – gained him instant support by members of the scientific community. Recognition of his work was reflected in the foundation of the Jennerian Society in London in 1803 by admirers in order to promote vaccination among the poor; Jenner was actively involved in its affairs. Government grants followed and Jenner carried out further experimental work on his vaccine. His interest in science led him to form a number of scientific societies and he was to become a Fellow of the Royal Society. Jenner was an active Freemason, serving in 1812 as Master of the Royal Lodge of Faith and Friendship, No. 270, based in Berkeley, Gloucestershire. This lodge was regularly visited by the Prince of Wales – the future George IV – and was a lodge that was to become associated with the Jenner family.[1]

The Defeat of Smallpox

Jenner was born in Berkeley in 1749 and had been inoculated against smallpox while at school. This inoculation, or variolation as it was termed, was a method of deliberately introducing smallpox to a person, thus giving them the disease so they could acquire immunity. It was a practice that carried its own risk of infection to others but was seen as safer than becoming infected with the disease during an outbreak. However, this variolation was to adversely affect his general health throughout his life and no doubt gave him the impetus to find an effective and safer method of immunity against the disease.

At thirteen Jenner was apprenticed to a local surgeon before going on to study surgery and anatomy under the celebrated surgeon John Hunter in

London, who became a lifelong friend. He returned to his native Berkeley in 1773 and set up a successful practice of his own. It was here in 1796 that Jenner made his observation that milkmaids who had caught the milder disease known as cowpox – which resulted in a blister rash mainly on the hands – seemed to be immune from the more aggressive and deadly smallpox.

To test his theory, Jenner had to experiment by introducing cowpox to someone who had not had smallpox, which he confidently did with James Phipps, the eight-year old son of his gardener. Jenner made a few scratches on the boy's arm and rubbed into them some infected material from the hands of a milkmaid, Sarah Nelmes, who had contracted cowpox. Jenner then introduced smallpox to the boy through the traditional variolation technique and, as predicted, the boy did not develop the disease. Jenner subsequently tested many other people with his vaccine, proving his theory that cowpox gave a greater immunity to smallpox.

Natural Philosophy

Edward Jenner was elected a Fellow of the Royal Society in 1789, not for his medical work but for his research on the study of the then misunderstood nesting habits of the cuckoo. Indeed, Jenner embraced the study of nature in a wider sense, examining many aspects of the natural world in order to gain a deeper understanding of what he saw as God's work. He was also an avid fossil-hunter and geologist: in 1819 he found a fossil of what would become known as the plesiosaur. At this time, a theory was developing that regarded fossils as the remains of species that could be extinct, a theory which Jenner came to support, saying that 'Fossils are…monuments to departed worlds'.

Fascinated by new ideas concerning any form of natural philosophy, Jenner had taken an interest in ballooning, launching his own balloon in 1784, which successfully flew a number of miles. He also enthusiastically studied the hibernation of animals during winter as well as the mystery of bird migration. He suggested that some birds left Britain for the winter and returned for the summer – a theory that contradicted the tradition that birds slept in mud for the winter.

He maintained an active correspondence with other eminent Freemasons of the period who shared his theories and ideas; Freemasons such as Sir Joseph Banks, a member of the Royal Somerset House and Inverness Lodge, No. 4, who served as president of the Royal Society,[2] and Erasmus

Darwin, initiated 1754 into Lodge St. Davids, No. 36 (S.C.), who was involved with the Birmingham-based Lunar Society, a number of whose members were Freemasons.[3]

The Royal Lodge of Faith and Friendship held a Science Select Lodge organised by Jenner where lodge members had to produce a paper on a specific scientific subject; this Science Select Lodge was reminiscent of the Lunar Society meetings. Other lectures had taken place within masonic lodges throughout the country, such as the Old Kings Arms Lodge, No. 28, London, the lectures being intricately entwined with the lodge meeting itself. Another example of scientific teaching taking place within lodges can be seen in the Lodge of Lights, No. 148, Warrington, which held lectures on Newtonian gravitational astronomy in 1800 and 1801. All three lodges are still working today.[4]

The Royal Lodge of Faith and Friendship continued to celebrate the life and work of Edward Jenner after his death in 1823 and other members of Jenner's family, such as his nephews Henry Jenner and the clergyman William Davies, became members. The lodge emblem, used to this day, commemorates the gift to Jenner of a wampum belt by the Five Nations of North America after Jenner personally sent them a sample of the cowpox virus along with a copy of his work on vaccination; Jenner wore this belt in front of his apron at the last masonic meeting he attended. In 1825, members of the Provincial Grand Lodge of Gloucestershire subscribed sufficient funds to erect a memorial statue to him in Gloucester Cathedral.[5]

Jenner certainly studied many aspects of the 'hidden mysteries of nature and science' and seemed to have found in Freemasonry a means by which he could convey his scientific beliefs as well as his spiritual and moralistic values. His studies of nature were firmly in balance with his belief in God's grand design of the universe. In a letter to his friend the Rev. Thomas Pruen, Jenner wrote:

> *'The weather may be inconvenient for the designs of man, but must always be in harmony with the designs of God, who has not only this planet, our Earth, to manage, but the universe. The whole creation is the work of God's hands. It cannot manage itself. Man cannot manage it, therefore, God is the manager.'*[6]

Joseph Brant: A Masonic legend

I was fascinated by the Masonic story of Joseph Brant, and as I wrote this article for *MQ Magazine* in October 2007, I remember showing the outline of the piece to Harald Braun, who was one of my PhD supervisors at the University of Liverpool, and he urged me to complete it as he also found Brant's story a fascinating one. For me, Brant's story reveals the true essence of brotherly love, which transcends war and conflict.

The story of Joseph Brant, the Mohawk 'American Indian' who fought for the Loyalists during the American War of Independence has been retold by the Iroquois peoples of the Six Nations and American Freemasons for centuries, and today Brant is featured in many Masonic Histories and is the topic of many websites. The story that is the most endearing is how Brant, a Mohawk chief, witnessed an American prisoner do a Masonic sign and spared the life of his fellow Mason. This action went down in history, and Brant became the embodiment of the 'noble savage' to Victorian England. This article will explain the events leading up to this event, and how Brant, in death, created even more controversy as the legends of his life grew and expanded.[7]

Brant was born in 1742 in the area around the banks of the Ohio River, his Indian name was Thayendanegea, meaning 'he places two bets' and as a child he was educated at Moor's Charity School for Indians in Lebanon, Connecticut, were he learned English and European History. He became a favourite of Sir William Johnson, who had taken Brant's sister Molly as a mistress, though they were married later after Johnson's wife died. Johnson was the British Superintendent for Northern Indian Affairs, and became close to the Mohawk people, and enlisted their allegiance in the French and Indian War of 1754-1763, with a young Brant taking up arms for the British.

After the war Brant found himself working as an interpreter

A portrait of Joseph Brant taken from the Memoir of Brant by William E. Palmer.

for Johnson. He had worked as an interpreter before the war and assisted in translating the prayer book and the Gospel of Mark into the Mohawk language, other translations included the Acts of the Apostles and a short history of the Bible, Brant having converted to Christianity, a religion which he embraced. Around 1775, after being appointed secretary to Sir William's successor, Guy Johnson, Brant received a Captain's commission in the British Army and set off for England, where he became a Freemason and confirmed his attachment to the British Crown. Brant was raised in Hiram's Cliftonian Lodge No. 814 in London, early in 1776, though his association with the Johnson's may have been an influence in his links to Freemasonry. Guy Johnson had accompanied Brant on his visit to England, the Johnson family having Masonic links. Hiram's Cliftonian Lodge had been founded in 1771, and during Brant's visit to the lodge, it had met at the Falcon in Princes Street, Soho. The lodge was erased in 1782. Brant's Masonic apron was, according to legend, presented to him by George III himself.

On his return to America, Brant became a key figure in securing the loyalty of other Iroquois tribes in fighting for the British against the 'rebels', and it was during the war that Joseph Brant entered into Masonic legend. After the surrender of the 'rebel' forces at the Battle of the Cedars on the St. Lawrence River in 1776, Brant famously saved the life of a certain Captain John McKinstry, a member of Hudson Lodge No.13 of New York, who was about to be burned at the stake. McKinstry, remembering that Brant was a Freemason, gave to him the Masonic sign of appeal which Brant recognized, an action which secured McKinstry's release and subsequent good treatment. McKinstry and Brant remained friends for life, and in 1805 he and Brant together visited the Masonic Lodge in Hudson, New York, where Brant was given an excellent reception. Brant's portrait now hangs in the lodge.

Another story relating to Brant during the war has another 'rebel' captive named Lieutenant Boyd giving Brant a Masonic sign, which secured him a reprieve from execution. However, on this occasion, Brant left his Masonic captive in the care of the British, who subsequently had Boyd tortured and executed. After the war, Brant removed himself with his tribe to Canada, establishing the Grand River Reservation for the Mohawk Indians. He became affiliated with Lodge No. 11 at the Mohawk village at Grand River of which he was the first Master and he later affiliated with Barton Lodge No.10 at Hamilton, Ontario. Brant returned to England in 1785 in an attempt to settle legal disputes on the Reservation lands, where he was again well received by George III and the Prince of Wales.

After Brant's death in 1807, his legend continued to develop, with numerous accounts of his life and his death being written. One such account lengthily entitled *The Life of Captain Joseph Brant with An Account of his Re-interment at Mohawk, 1850, and of the Corner Stone Ceremony in the Erection of the Brant Memorial, 1886,* celebrated Brant's achievements and detailed that a certain Jonathan Maynard had also been saved by Brant during the war. Like McKinstry, Maynard, who later became a member of the Senate of Massachusetts, had been saved

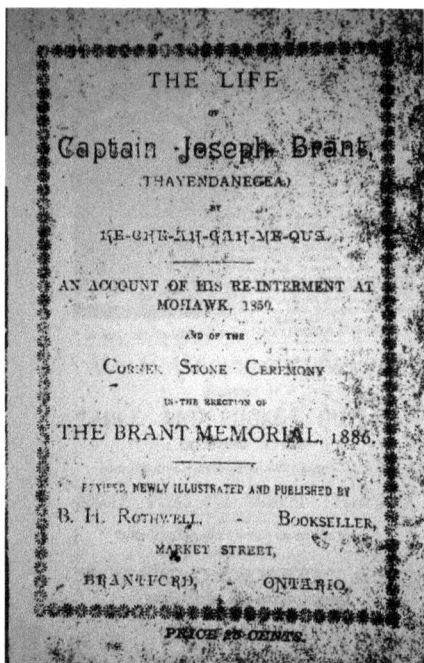

The title page of a pamphlet describing the corner stone ceremony in the erection of the Brant memorial, 1886.

at the last minute by Brant who had recognized him giving a Masonic sign. Brant's remains were re-interred in 1850 with an Indian relay, were a number of Warriors took turn in carrying his remains to the Chapel of the Mohawks, located in Brant's Mohawk Village which is now part of the city of Brantford. Many local Freemasons were present, and his tomb was restored with an inscription paid for by them.

The legend of Brant saving his fellow Masons was examined by Albert C. Mackey in his *Encyclopedia of Freemasonry* in which he referred to a book entitled *Indian Masonry* by a certain Brother Robert C. Wright. In the book, Wright states that *'signs given by the Indians could easily be mistaken for Masonic signs by an enthusiastic Freemason'.* Using Wright's claims that the Indians used similar Masonic signs or gestures within their culture, and these were mistaken by over enthusiastic Freemasons, Mackey was putting forward an argument that the stories of encounters with 'Masonic' Indians were perhaps in doubt. Mackey then put forward the question *'is the Indian a Freemason'* before examining a number of historically Native American Indians that were Freemasons, including Joseph Brant and General Eli S. Parker, the Seneca Chief who fought in the American Civil War. Mackey concluded that *'Thus from primitive and ancient rites akin to Freemasonry, which had their origin in the shadows of the distant past, the American Indian is graduating into Free and Accepted Masonry as it has been taught to us. It is an instructive example of the universality of human belief in fraternity, morality and immortality'*. Mackey presented that the Indians, in recognizing the Universal ethos of Freemasonry within their own culture, were drawn to the Craft. Thus an understanding into Brant's moralistic approach to fellow Freemasons who were prisoners during the war was being sought, his actions fascinating Masonic historians well into the twentieth century.

Brant became a symbol for Freemasonry, his story being used as a metaphor for the Masonic bond, a bond which became greater than the bond of serving ones country during wartime. Brant also came to represent a respect for the Native American Indian during a time when the USA was promoting the 'manifest destiny', an ethos which the United States government saw as God's right for them to settle the Indian lands of the west. Brant's myth even exceeded the traditional Victorian image of the 'noble savage', his meeting of other Freemasons while visiting London such as the writer James Boswell and Masonic members of the Hanoverian Household such as the Prince of Wales compounded this. Brant once said *'My principle is founded on justice, and justice is all I wish for'*, a statement which certainly conveyed his moralistic and Masonic ethos.[8]

Sir Thomas Stamford Raffles; Singapore and Freemasonry

This article, which appeared in *Freemasonry Today* in summer 2010, conveyed an anti-slavery theme, which reflected an earlier article I did on how certain Freemasons became involved in the abolition movement. Some Freemasons however, particularly in a number of Liverpool lodges at the time, were directly involved in slavery, so the attitudes of Freemasons were certainly not clear cut on the issue of slavery. I explored these issues deeper in a chapter of my book *The Transformation of Freemasonry*, which was published in 2010.

The ethos of Freemasonry has never been so best exemplified than when a member of the society can make good from bad, and Sir Thomas Stamford Raffles did just that; from the lust of Empire building that was franticly taking place during the early nineteenth century, Raffles not only founded a city when he established Singapore, but he founded an international trading centre. He created churches and schools for the indigenous population, allowed local businesses to operate, outlawed slavery in the city, and drafted the first constitution of the new Singapore, taking a complete moralistic stance on its development.

Sir Thomas Stamford Raffles was born on the 6th of July 1781, on the Ship *Ann*, off the harbour of Port Morant in Jamaica. He was the only surviving son of Benjamin Raffles, a captain trading in the West Indies. As a child Raffles was sent to an Academy at Hammersmith, then, at the age of 14 he became an employee of the East India Company, working as a clerk at East India House in London, an event which was to determine the rest of his relatively short life. Raffles held high ambitions, and he gained the post of Assistant Secretary in Penang, and with a large increase in salary, he then married his first wife Olivia before setting out for Southeast Asia in 1805. He had a passion for knowledge, and learned the Malayan language on the voyage.

This new position opened up a new world for Raffles and he entered into the sphere of colonial networking, finally joining Freemasonry in July 1812, in the *Lodge Virtutis et Artis Amici*, in Buitenzorg, Java, under the Grand Orient of the Netherlands. He was subsequently raised in the *Lodge De Vriendschap* in Surabaya, Java, in July 1813, serving as Worshipful Master the same year. His close friend and associate Thomas McQuoid was also a Freemason and a founder of the *Lodge Neptune* which was based in Penang and McQuoid was 'Perfected' with Raffles in *Rose Croix Chapter*

La Vertueuse in Batavia in 1816. Thomas McQuoid became a longtime friend and business partner of Raffles, supporting him in key decisions as his confidant.[9]

Raffles' wife had died in 1814, and certain charges had been made against him regarding mismanagement and improperly purchasing land. Raffles also succumbed to Ill health – something which plagued him during his career in Southeast Asia - and forced him to leave Java and return to England on the 25th of March of 1816, just after his 'Perfection'.

On his journey home, Raffles stopped off at St. Helena, meeting Napoleon, referring to him as a *'monster'*. Back in England, with his health recovered, he remarried; he was made a Fellow of the Royal Society, published his work *The History of Java* and was knighted, receiving support from Princess Charlotte, the daughter of the Prince Regent – the future George IV. Raffles was celebrated while in London, the charges against him were dropped, and he was offered the position of Lieutenant General of Bencoolen – a British garrison located in south west Sumatra.

He took up the position and after arriving at Bencoolen, with renewed confidence he immediately set about bringing in new reforms. In 1818 he passed a new 'Regulation' that would bring about the eventual abolition of slavery in the area and banned cockfighting. The slave trade had been abolished in Britain in 1807, but slaves were still kept throughout British colonies, such as the West Indies and throughout settlements in Asia. Even after the Slavery Abolition Act of 1833, the territories of the East India Company remained exempt. English Freemasons had been as divided on the issue of slavery as much as the population of England had been, with some Freemasons – especially in the port of Liverpool – such as merchant Thomas Golightly and Liverpool MP Sir Isaac Gascoyne, openly supporting the slave trade before its abolition in 1807. Internationally, divisions on the issue of slavery were still evident among Freemasons, most famously with the American brethren; with George Washington keeping slaves, and Benjamin Franklin being an ardent abolitionist.[10]

Raffles had a moralistic passion which drove him on to introduce new reforms in the new colonies liberalizing the severe Dutch colonial system and to curb Dutch expansion in Southeast Asia. He was overtly anti-slavery and held a modern vision for the governance of Bencoolen; he had sent fellow Freemason and politician George Canning a memorandum which set out his aims – especially mentioning the idea of establishing a station at the eastern exit of the straits of Malacca before the Dutch did. The Dutch were always a problem to the British in Southeast Asia, and Singapore, which became the hub for the British Empire in Southeast Asia, was to be free of Dutch influence.

George Canning was a supporter for the abolition of slavery, and was at the time serving as the President of the Board of Control, an office that was responsible for overseeing the East India Company, and thus Canning was very much interested in British influence in South East Asia. Canning had become a Freemason in 1810 and he joined two of the most prestigious lodges in London; Lodge No. 4 which was one of the four original lodges that had formed the 'Premier/Modern' Grand Lodge of 1717, and the Prince of Wales Lodge No. 259, the membership of which included the Prince of Wales himself. Canning was a well-connected gentleman, and was also a member of a number of clubs in London such as Whites, giving an ambitious politician such as Canning a nexus of powerful contacts.[11]

Raffles became intensely involved in the settlement and administration of Singapore from 1819; partly surveying the island, setting out plans for settlement, establishing places of education and worship and in 1823, he drafted the constitution of Singapore, specifically prohibiting slavery and gaming – following his moralistic stance which he had practiced in the administration of Bencoolen. Tragedy had struck while Raffles was in Bencoolen when, after an outbreak of dysentery, he lost three of his children. His own health had suffered once more, and after finalising the constitution of Singapore, he set off on his final journey for England.

He finally returned to England on 22 Aug 1824, over a year after he left Singapore, founding the Zoological Society of London in Apr 1826, along with various members of the nobility, clergy, eminent naturalists and gentlemen, some of whom were also Fellows of the Royal Society. Raffles had always been interested in making notes of the plants and animal life of Southeast Asia – but most of his specimens and effects were destroyed in a fire on a ship as Raffles set off for England. He became its first chairman and president, and his zeal for zoology and botany – and indeed the promotion of them as a science, is in tune with Raffles' passion for education.

Raffles died of apoplexy, a day before his 45th birthday on the 5th of July, 1826. He had been suffering from bouts of illness for some years. Because of his anti-slavery stance, he was refused burial inside his local parish church, St. Mary's in Hendon, by the vicar, whose family had made its money in the slave trade. Stamford Raffles was an extraordinary man, his courage in banning slavery from the colonies under his jurisdiction, and his zeal for education testifying to his modern outlook. It is no wonder that in parts of Southeast Asia today, he is celebrated through Freemasonry.

Lodges connected to Raffles

The Dutch Freemasons were probably the first to set up an organized lodge in the Far East, but the beginnings of Singapore's Lodge is traced to the founding of Freemasonry in the Eastern Archipelago. This began with the establishment of the Lodge at Bencoolen in 1765. Raffles certainly attended a number of lodges in the region - *Lodge Virtutis et Artis Amici*, in Buitenzorg, Java, *Lodge de Vriendschap* in Surabaya and *Chapter La Vertueuse* in Batavia. Such was the influence of Raffles that the local Lodge bears his name and coat of arms as their insignia.

Freemasonry in Singapore began with the first 'mother' lodge, *Lodge Zetland in the East No. 748 E.C* established and consecrated on the 8th of December 1845, in a house at Armenian Street. At that first lodge meeting, twelve leading members of the small European community in Singapore - among them senior lawyer, William Napier, deputy superintendent of police, Thomas Dunman and Straits Times editor, Robert Carr Woods - were proposed for initiation. On the 15th of December 1845, William Napier became the first initiated Brother, next was prominent citizen Mr. William H. Read followed by soldier, Lieutenant Benjamin Bloomfield Keane. Other notable Freemasons in Singapore's early history included the first attorney-general, Thomas Braddell; Rajah of Sarawak, James Brooke, Admiral Henry Keppel, John Coulson Smith, former headmaster of Raffles Institution, and Thomas Owen Crane, Justice of Peace, and trustee of Raffles Institution. The Masonic Hall in Singapore was built in 1879, and was known locally as the 'Haunted House' as the local people misunderstood the ceremonies that went on there.[12]

Elizabeth Aldworth - The First Lady Freemason

I wrote this article after being invited to give a talk a lodge in Cork, Ireland, in May, 2014. The Masonic Hall in Cork had a number of artefacts regarding Elizabeth Aldworth as a Lady Mason, and celebrated the connection with her portrait in the Hall. I also visited her memorial in St. Finbarr's Cathedral in Cork. This article was subsequently published in *The Square*, in September 2014.

In an exposé of the later eighteenth century called *Jachin and Boaz*, there is an interesting mention of a lodge in Ireland that admitted a woman, the anonymous author of the work stating that she was '*as good a Mason as any of them*'.[13] On a recent visit to Cork where I was giving a talk to Lodge No.555, I had the opportunity to find out more about this mysterious Lady Freemason as to my surprise, the Cork Masonic Hall still celebrated the connection to this enigmatic figure. A portrait of the Lady Freemason hangs in the dining room of the Masonic Hall, along with what is believed to be her

Lady Mason
(Masonic Hall, Cork)

apron and a special jewel that supposedly belonged to her, and a *Memoir of the Lady Freemason* was actually published in the early nineteenth century in Cork. So who was this Lady Mason? And is the story true?

The Lady Freemason is named as the Hon. Elizabeth Aldworth, born in 1693, the daughter of Arthur St. Leger, first Viscount Doneraile, who was said to have held a lodge in his home at Doneraile Court, County Cork. According to the *Memoir*, it was at one of these lodge meetings that Elizabeth overheard the activities of the lodge while reading in the library room next door. Some of the bricks from the dividing wall between the library and the room where the lodge was meeting could be removed, so Elizabeth was able to watch the lodge proceedings through the narrow gap. After watching the meeting and understanding the importance of the secret nature of the ceremony she had witnessed, Elizabeth then tried to escape the library be leaving through a door that would lead through the far end of the room where the lodge was held, and, if she was quiet enough, she hoped she could escape without notice.[14]

However, on turning the handle and opening the door, she was confronted by her father's butler who was acting as Tyler, and after raising an alarm, she was 'detained' in the library. The Brethren of the lodge then discussed what best to do; their secrets had been revealed and the mysteries of their workings may have been under threat, so a decision was made to make Elizabeth a Freemason. The date of her initiation can only be speculated upon, as there are no actual lodge records and no actual mention of Elizabeth at any other lodge meeting, but a date between 1710-1712 is presented in the new edition of the *Memoir*. Elizabeth married Richard Aldworth of Newmarket Court at St. Finbarr's in Cork in 1713, and she died in 1775.[15]

The actual evidence for the Lady Freemason is, on the whole, rather slim to put it bluntly, but there is a mention of a recorded testimony by a certain Arundel Hill Esq., of Graig, Cork, who claimed that he was at her initiation and sat with her in the lodge. However, this comes from a later document that only dates to 1862, well after the event. There is also the apron of the Lady Freemason, which had been preserved as an heirloom at Newmarket Court, and there is a miniature portrait of Elizabeth with the aforementioned Masonic jewel, which is also now held at Cork Masonic Hall, though this has been dated to the early nineteenth century. There were early lodges recorded in County Cork, and there was of course the independent Grand Lodge of Munster which operated between 1726-1735, but no record of Elizabeth at a lodge has yet come to light.

Elizabeth was buried at St. Finbarr's Cathedral in Cork, and a brass memorial plaque was placed there later by the Aldworth family which celebrates her as a Freemason and as being initiated in 1712 into Lodge No. 44 held at Doneraile Court. Lodge No.44 however, is only recorded as existing at Doneraile in the later eighteenth century, though it has been speculated in the new edition of the *Memoir* that this lodge could have been a successor to the Lady Freemason's older unwarranted Mother Lodge. Despite the lack of contemporary records, the belief in the Lady Freemason of Cork is as strong as ever.[16]

So, we end were we began; an enigmatic story of a Lady Mason who was described as being '*as good a Mason as any of them*', a statement that echoes the original *Memoir* of 1811, which declares:

'*...she lived up to the highest principles of the Order to which she belonged. Possessed of considerable wealth, her purse and influence were always at the* *command of any Brother in distress and to all appeals she responded with ready sympathy and large-hearted generosity...she was a most exemplary Mason and headed her Lodge frequently in procession...She had such a veneration for Masonry that she would never suffer it to be lightly spoken of in her hearing...'*[17]

Viscount Combermere; War Hero, Freemason and the mystery of the moving coffins

This article was published in *Freemasonry Today* in the winter 2010/2011 issue, and reflected my interest in charismatic figures who became prominent in English Freemasonry as the nineteenth century progressed. I had also stumbled across the story of the 'moving coffins' of Barbados in a book by Arthur C. Clarke, so I combined the two elements of Combermere's story, which made for an entertaining read with a Masonic context.

High ranking charismatic figures became essential to Freemasonry, especially after the dark difficult years of the early nineteenth century that some lodges had experienced. These influential figures attracted aspiring social-climbing men to the lodges that they were associated with, playing a part in making the Craft popular again. One such charismatic figure was Viscount Combermere, who became Provincial Grand Master of Cheshire in 1830. Combermere became an active and extremely popular high ranking Freemason, following in the footsteps of his father Sir Robert S. Cotton, who had also served as Provincial Grand Master of Cheshire from 1785-1810. Stapleton Stapleton-Cotton, 1st Viscount Combermere was a war hero, having fought in the Peninsula Wars, and was a close friend of the Duke of Wellington, who was also a Freemason. He had served as commander of Wellington's cavalry, earning a reputation for fearless bravery and received the personal thanks from Wellington himself.

Combermere renovated his home at Combermere Abbey in Cheshire extensively and constructed the 'Wellington Wing' especially to commemorate the Duke's visit to the house in 1820. His popularity as a local war hero was evident when the Provincial Grand Lodge met in Macclesfield in 1852, where the procession route to the meeting place at the Macclesfield Arms Hotel was crammed with *'flags and banners'*, and in front of the Hotel *'a lofty triumphal arch of evergreens was erected, from which depended banners bearing 'Welcome Combermere' and 'Salamanca'.* When the Provincial Grand Lodge met n Congleton in 1855, Combermere again received a rapturous hero's welcome, the public celebrations for the arrival of this *'Cheshire Hero'* being ecstatic:

> *'From early morn the bells of St. Peter's Church rang out their merry peals; from church tower, hall, public buildings, factories, and private dwellings waved innumerable flags…on small bannerets appeared the words 'Cheshire Hero,' 'Peninsula,' 'Bhurtpoor'.*

Combermere's standing among the Masonic community of Cheshire was so great that he was toasted as *'The Hero of Cheshire'* at the Provincial Grand Lodge, and his son Wellington Cotton, followed in his footsteps becoming a high ranking Mason within the Cheshire Province. On the death of the Duke of Wellington in 1852, Combermere gave a speech to the Provincial Grand Lodge, in which he said:

> *'He had been associated with him (Wellington) since 1793. Perhaps it was not generally known that the Duke was a Mason, he was made in Ireland, and often when in Spain, where Masonry was prohibited, in conversation with his Lordship, he regretted repeatedly how sorry he was that his military duties had prevented him taking the active part his feelings dictated, for it was his opinion that Masonry was a great and royal art, beneficial to the individual and to the community.'*

The Duke of Wellington's Masonic career had begun in 1790, when he entered into his family lodge in Ireland, but after 1795 he distanced himself from the Craft, and even opposed Masonic processions and meetings when in Lisbon, Portugal in 1810, realising it was sensitive to the local population. Despite this, as the speech by Combermere testified, Wellington's links to the Craft were known, and in 1838, he was asked by his old lodge in Ireland for his permission to rename the lodge after him, though he declined to give it.

Like Viscount Combermere, many British war heroes became popular leaders of Freemasonry as the nineteenth century progressed, another example being the charismatic Troop Sergeant Major Richard Hall Williams who was one of the 'noble six hundred' in the infamous charge of the light brigade in 1854. Williams became a leading Freemason founding the Worsley Lodge No. 1814 in 1880 and served as its first Worshipful Master. Another Crimean war hero who became an influential Freemason was Robert Loyd-Lindsay, 1st Baron Wantage, who was awarded the Victoria Cross and became involved in numerous lodges, Loyd-Lindsay going on to be a prominent figure within the United Grand Lodge of England. The importance of these war heroes within nineteenth century English Freemasonry suggests an arcane attraction to the enigmatic masculine figures of Empire; in drawing the celebrities of the period, be it aristocracy, war heroes or alluring local industrialists and professionals, Masonry would hold appeal to aspirant young men.

After the Napoleonic wars, Combermere was appointed as Governor of Barbados in 1817, and it was in Barbados that an infamous incident occurred that has since made Combermere the focus of many a book on the paranormal. The macabre 'moving coffins of Barbados' have been discussed and researched by countless paranormal investigators, the incident causing such a stir on the island in 1819 that Combermere himself became directly involved. The incident centred on the tomb of the Chase family, a vault which lies in the graveyard of Christ Church in Oistins, situated in the south-west of Barbados.

The curious events had actually started a number of years before with the burial of Mrs Thomasina Goddard in 1807. The tomb however had been there for nearly a century before; being the resting place for a certain Honourable James Elliott who was buried there in 1724, but by the time of Mrs Goddard's burial, his coffin had vanished. A few months after Mrs Goddard's burial, the tomb was reopened to bury Mary Ann Chase, the infant daughter of the Hon. Thomas Chase, a local plantation owner. In the 6th of July 1812, the tomb was again reopened for the burial of another daughter, and the following month, Thomas Chase himself passed away and the tomb was reopened once more.

This time however, when the tomb was opened, the tiny lead coffins of his children were found to have mysteriously and inexplicably moved; especially the coffin of Mary Ann which appeared to have been thrown from one side of the tomb to the other, leaning head down in the corner. Later, when another infant was buried, the coffins were again displaced and strewn around the tomb. The burial a few weeks after of Samuel Brewster, who had been murdered by slaves, revealed further disarray, with the coffins again having been mysteriously moved around. By the time yet another burial took place on the 7th of July, 1819, the nervous locals had an idea of what to find, and sure enough the tomb was yet again in a mess; predictably the coffins had been moved again and the coffin of Mrs Goddard had been completely smashed.

Rumour and superstition spread through the community and crowds gathered around the tomb to see the unearthly chaos, and it was then that Combermere himself became involved, personally supervising the investigation into how the disturbances occurred; checking for secret tunnels and placing the coffins neatly in order again – recording the layout with a sketch. When the slab was replaced to conceal the entrance of the tomb, Combermere made a series of secret marks and symbols within the cement to alert him to further tampering.

Ten months later, Combermere and some friends returned to the tomb to check on the outcome of their investigation, and sure enough after carefully opening the tomb, the coffins were again in chaos; the children's coffins having been thrown to the back of the vault. Nothing had been disturbed on the outside of the tomb, the appearance being perfect and Combermere's secret marks still being visible. Another sketch of the coffins in their chaotic state was done to record the event and the vault was closed once more. The mystery was never solved.

Diagrams of the moving coffins

Max Montesole and Albert Calvert (care of the Authors' Lodge)

Conan Doyle, Kipling, Rider Haggard, Jerome K Jerome and the Authors' Lodge

This article was my last piece commissioned by Michael Baigent, who was editor of *Freemasonry Today*, and it was finally published in the autumn 2011 issue. I was deeply interested in the history of the Authors' Lodge, especially with its early connection to the Authors' Club. I subsequently got to know a number of the current members of the lodge and still receive a summons to visit.

> *'Once a priest, always a priest; once a mason, always a mason; but once a journalist, always and forever a journalist.'*
> Freemason Rudyard Kipling, *A Matter of Fact, Many Inventions*, 1893.

There is a Masonic lodge which still meets in London called the Authors' Lodge No.3456, which, when founded in November 1910, received letters of goodwill from 'Brothers' Sir Arthur Conan Doyle, Henry Rider Haggard, Rudyard Kipling, and Jerome K. Jerome. Rudyard Kipling, had been initiated into Freemasonry in the Hope and Perseverance Lodge No.782, based in Lahore, India, in 1886, and went on to become an honorary member of the Authors' Lodge. The lodge had a direct connection to the London based Authors' Club, which had been founded in 1891, being constituted by the Masonic members of the Authors' Club, founders such as Max Montesole and A.F. Calvert, who had famously discovered an early

Masonic *Catechism* dating from the early eighteenth century, which he eventually sold to Masonic historian Douglas Knoop. The consecration of the Authors' Lodge reveals the intricate relationships between certain gentlemen's clubs and Freemasonry; the founding of the lodge being seen as not only a way of promoting the Authors' Club amongst Freemasons, but also providing a means of promoting Freemasonry within the club, attracting literary men into the Craft *'could not fail to add lustre to the Order.'*

Kipling and Rider Haggard were very close friends, and they both famously conveyed Freemasonry in their work. Indeed, Masonic themes can be seen in Rider Haggard's late Victorian works *King Solomon's Mines* and the wonderfully exotic novel *She*, a story which deals with death and re-birth. Both of these works present the idea of the heroic explorer searching lost civilisations for hidden knowledge and, along with Kipling's *The Man Who Would Be King*, testify not only to the popularity of Freemasonry at the time, but also the acceptance of the Craft in Victorian society, which, within these literary contexts also conveyed an element of mystery and the occult. Rider Haggard was also a close friend of Egyptologist and occultist Ernest A. Wallis Budge, both of them, along with Kipling, being celebrated members of the literary Savile Club.

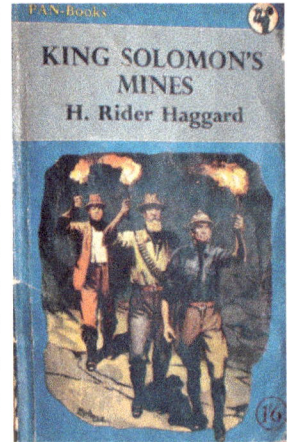

Victorian gentlemen's clubs - popular amongst the literary gentlemen of the time, had links to Freemasonry during the period. Indeed, many Victorian writers, artists and politicians were members of both, the thriving social scene offering networking and social advancement, both Freemasonry and the clubs having similar dining etiquette, strict dress codes and rules on balloting for new members. The networking that took place in the London clubs attracted the vivid imagination of Victorian writers, some of whom even wrote about their experiences of the mysterious activities that occurred behind the closed doors. Arthur Conan Doyle, who was initiated into the Pheonix Lodge, No.257, at Southsea, Hampshire, on the 26th of January, 1887, made a literary reference to a London gentleman's club in his 1893 Sherlock Holmes short story *The Adventure of the Greek Interpreter*, were Sherlock Holmes visits his brother Mycroft at the mysterious 'Diogenes Club' which he describes as:

'the queerest club in London' being for gentlemen *'who have no wish for the company of their fellows. Yet they are not averse to comfortable chairs and the latest periodicals.'*

The bizarre rules of the club are described:

'No member is permitted to take the least notice of any other one. Save in the Strangers' Room, no talking is, under any circumstances, permitted, and three offences, if brought to the notice of the committee, render the talker liable to expulsion. My brother (Mycroft) was one of the founders, and I have myself found it a very soothing atmosphere.'

The location of the club in the story was given as being on Pall Mall, a short distance from the Carlton Club, Conan Doyle presenting its interior as having a games room and *'a large and luxurious'* reading room. The 'Diogenes Club' was fictional, but with Mycroft's secretive career in government, the club was presented as having possible deeper mysterious political agendas. Conan Doyle was obviously being inspired by the secrecy and mysterious nature of such gentlemen's clubs, so it is not surprising that he also occasionally referred to Freemasonry in his Sherlock Holmes stories, such as in *The Red-Headed League*, when Holmes – who was obviously very familiar with Masonic symbolism - recognised that a certain gentleman was a Freemason, the particular gentleman being surprised that Holmes knew of his membership:

'I won't insult your intelligence by telling you how I read that, especially as, rather against the strict rules of your order, you use an arc and compass breastpin.'

He also referred to Freemasonry in other Sherlock Holmes stories, such as *The Adventure of the Norwood Builder* and *The Adventure of the Retired Colourman*, as well as mentioning Freemasonry in his other works.

Conan Doyle, along with other Victorian Freemasons, such as Arthur Edward Waite, had embraced psychic research, an interest that developed after the death of his wife and several other close family members, and until his death in 1930, he ardently supported spiritualism and constantly sought proof of life after death, a curiosity which can be somewhat paralleled with writer and Freemason Mark Twain's interest in parapsychology in the USA. Conan Doyle's 1926 work *The History of Spiritualism* also lent his support to séances conducted by various psychics at the time and their supposed spiritual materialisations. One of the spiritualists that Conan Doyle supported was Daniel Douglas Home. Fellow Freemason Lord Lindsay was also a supporter of Home, having witnessed the spiritualist mysteriously levitate out of a third story window only to return through the window of an adjoining room.

Jerome K. Jerome's Masonic membership is hotly debated, though he certainly mixed in Masonic circles; Jerome having been good friends with fellow writers and Freemasons Conan Doyle, Rider Haggard and Kipling. Jerome was a member of the Authors' Club, which included other illustrious and literary Freemasons such as Oscar Wilde and Winston Churchill. Conan Doyle was Chairman of the Authors' Club for many years, often reading his manuscripts to members prior to publication, and one of the founders of the club was the writer and Freemason Sir Walter Besant, who went on to be a founder of the celebrated Quatuor Coronati Lodge No.2076, in 1894 - the London based lodge dedicated to Masonic research.

Jerome also contributed to a Masonic publication; a souvenir of the Grand Masonic Bazaar in aid of the Annuity Fund of Scottish Masonic Benevolence in 1890. The publication, given the rather humorous title of *Pot Pourri of Gifts Literal and Artistic*, included the lost classic Jerome story *The Prince's Quest*, a rare and much sought after piece of Jerome literature. *The Prince's Quest* is a fairytale which tells the beautiful story of a Prince who is searching for love; after traveling the length and breadth of the land on his quest, he returns home to his empty court, only to find love has been waiting there all along in the guise of a fair maiden.

Along with this contribution to the Masonic publication and the reference to him and his 'Brothers' writing a letter of goodwill to the Authors' Lodge, Jerome's Masonic membership has been regularly discussed and debated over the years. The Preface of *Pot Pourri of Gifts Literal and Artistic* puts forward that many of its contributors were not members of the Craft, though it does say *'charity claims us all in a common brotherhood'*. The preface was written by the artist William Grant Stevenson who was the Master of Lodge of Dramatic and Arts No. 757, which still meets in Edinburgh and was founded in 1888. The publication was produced by the Lodge Dramatic and Arts for the fund-raising bazaar held in Edinburgh in December 1890.

Jerome used the setting of a gentleman's club as the location of a story which had been told to the narrator in his 1909 work *The Philosopher's Joke*, and he seemed well acquainted with the social etiquette and aesthetic atmosphere of the clubs. Jerome also spiritually commented on Freemason Rider Haggard's work in his essay *Dreams*. Jerome's Masonic membership is still debated as there is a lack of Masonic records which refer to him, but there is still a wealth of evidence which suggests that he had links to the Craft and was aware of Freemasonry. He certainly mixed in Masonic circles and was a member of gentleman's clubs, having been influenced by them in his writing. Being friends with Conan Doyle, Rider Haggard and Kipling, Jerome would have been familiar with Freemasonry, and would have found it an interesting social activity. Perhaps future findings may reveal more about his Masonic membership. Their letters of goodwill testifies their respect for the founding of the Authors' Lodge, a lodge which is celebrating its centenary this year.

Sex, Seduction, and Secret Societies: Byron, the Carbonari and Freemasonry

I first presented this paper at the International Byron Conference, at the International University of Venice in July 2007. It wasn't until I presented the paper to the Ars Macionica Lodge at the Regular Grand Lodge of Belgium in May 2017, that it was finally published in their transactions *Acta Macionica*, Vol.27, (2017). The paper was also presented to the International Masonic Conference, Athens, Greece in the same year, and was subsequently published in a number of Masonic magazines around the world, including the November/December 2018 edition of Montana Freemason.

The eighteeneth century was a period which witnessed the development of English Freemasonry as a social phenomenon, with the society undrergoing constant transitions, modernisations and rebellions. The society had split into two main rival factions in 1751, with two grand lodges existing, the Moderns and the Antients, and as a result the society expanded, with Masonic lodges by both organisations being founded throughout England, Europe and the American colonies. The influence of the society on artists, writers and free thinkers was immense, and this paper will examine the influence of the Craft on one particular writer and revolutionary, the Romantic poet George Gordon Byron, the 6th Baron Byron.

George Gordon Byron was born in 1788, and is regarded as a leading figure in the Romantic movement as well as one of Britains greatest poets. Byron also became known for his scandelous lifestyle, aristocratic excesses, and sexual and social intrigues, but even though he was not a Freemason, he did, as we shall see, have rather deep rooted connections to the society. After the publication of his first epic poem *Childe Harold's Pilgramage* in 1812, Byron was, for a time, the toast of Regency London; he was elected to the most exclusive of gentlemen's

George Gordon Byron, the 6th Baron Byron.

24

clubs, he had affairs with desirable women, an affiar with Lady Caroline Lamb led her to label him with the imortal line '*Mad, bad and dangerous to know*'. Byron also took an interest in the same sex and was rumoured to have had an affair with his half sister. The scandals, rumours and gossip led to him leaving England for good in 1816.

Freemasonry certainly fascinated another writer who was linked to the Romantic movement; Thomas de Quincey, also known as the Opium Eater after his auto-biographical work that detailed his addiction to laudanum. De Quincey wrote the *Origin of the Rosicrucians and the Free-Masons* which was first published in January 1824, a work that attempted to examine the origins of these entwined secret societies. Though de Quincey was not a Mason, like Byron, he was aware of Freemasonry, the history and the nature of secret societies providing a profound interest. De Quincey, like the poets William Blake and Samuel Taylor Coleridge, also drew inspiration from the works of Emmanuel Swedenborg, the Swedish visionary who later lent his name to the Masonic Swedenborgian Rite.[18] Freemasonry certainly attracted poets such as Robert Burns, a Scottish Mason who is often observed as a pioneer of the Romantic Movement.

The Poet and artist William Blake was also influenced by Freemasonry in his artwork, incorporating what can be interpreted as Masonic themes in works such as *Newton* and *The Ancient of Days*.[19] Another writer and friend of Byron's who was a Freemason was Dr John William Polidori. Polidori was Byron's personal physician who wrote the short Gothic story *The Vampyre*, which was the first ever published Vampire story in English. The story was based on Byron's *Fragment of a Novel* – a story composed at the Villa Diodati by Lake Geneva in Switzerland in June 1816, during the same time Mary Shelley produced what would later develop into *Frankenstein*. Polidori became a Freemason in 1818,[20] his story being published the following year.[21]

The 'Wicked Lord'

Byron's great uncle, the eccentric fifth Lord Byron, had been Grand Master of the 'Premier' or 'Modern' Grand Lodge from 1747-51, and it may have been through him that the poet developed a familiarity with the themes of Freemasonry. As we shall see, Byron mentioned Freemasonry in his poetry, and commonly celebrated classical architecture in his work, discussing the many Temples of antiquity. Byron, who had been on the Grand Tour, continuously praised the lost knowledge of the ancient world, and in his epic poem *Childe Harold's Pilgrimage*, he attacked Lord Elgin for his plunder of the Parthenon, and expressed the hidden mysteries held within the classical Temples:

> *'Here let me sit upon this massy stone,*
> *The marble column's yet unshaken base!*
> *Here, son of Saturn! Was thy favourite throne:*
> *Mightiest of many such! Hence let me trace*
> *The latent grandeur of thy dwelling-place.*
> *It may not be: nor even can Fancy's eye*
> *Restore what Time hath labour'd to deface.*
> *Yet these proud pillars claim no passing sigh;*
> *Unmoved the Moslem sits, the light Greek carols by.'* [22]

A Temple displayed in an edition of Byron's epic poem
Childe Harold's Pilgrimage.

Byron's great uncle, the 'Wicked Lord', hosted regular ritualistic weekend parties on his estate Newstead Abbey, in a somewhat similar fashion to Sir Francis Dashwood's Hell Fire and Dilettanti meetings at West Wycombe. The 'Wicked Lord' was a rather clubbable gentleman, being involved in an aristocratic dining club which met in the Star and Garter Tavern in London. However, true to his wild nature, he killed his neighbor William Chaworth during an argument, who was also a fellow member of his club, resulting in a murder trial in the House of Lords in 1765. He was eventually found guilty of manslaughter and, after the payment of a fine, he was a free man, though as a result of the scandal became a recluse, living in debt with his mistress in the decaying Gothic splendor of Newstead Abbey. [23] He certainly had a profound influence on his heir, the inheritance of the Gothic Abbey supplying a haunting and melancholy inspiration to the poet.

According to H.J. Whymper writing in *AQC*, the 'Wicked Lord' had been a popular and a somewhat charismatic Grand Master, and his absence during six out of ten Grand Lodge meetings was attributed to being on business out of the country. During his term as Grand Master he showed none of the temper or eccentricity of his later years, and the minutes of the Grand Lodge during his office revealed a Grand Master who was far from 'Wicked'.[24] Whymper was indeed sympathetic to Byron's Grand Mastership, and dismissed Gould's view of the 'Wicked Lord', Gould having written that *'the affairs of the Society were much neglected, and to this period of misrule, aggravated by the summary erasure of numerous lodges, we must look, I think, for the cause of that organized rebellion against authority, resulting in the great Schism.'* Gould clearly placing the blame for the formation of the 'Antients' with Byron.[25] Whymper put forward that Byron's image was certainly tainted after his conviction of manslaughter, leading to his *'unpopularity'* being *'improperly seized upon to account for the dissensions in the Craft...'*[26]

Lord Byron, Don Juan, the Carbonari and Revolution

Byron was certainly aware of Freemasonry, though he mentioned it only twice in his epic poem *Don Juan*. He first commented on the aristocratic networking aspects of the Craft in Canto XIII, Verse XXIV:

> *'And thus acquaintance grew at noble routs*
> *And diplomatic dinners or at other –*
> *For Juan stood well both with Ins and Outs,*
> *As in Freemasonry a higher brother.*
> *Upon his talent Henry had no doubts;*
> *His manner showed him sprung from a higher mother,*
> *And all men like to show their hospitality,*
> *To him whose breeding matched with this quality.'* [27]

Byron seemed to be referring to the hierarchical system of Freemasonry, which at Grand Lodge level, was dominated by the gentry and led by certain charismatic aristocrats, Don Juan being portrayed as moving in well-connected and well-bred circles. He then touched upon the Craft once more in Canto XIV, Verse XXII of the same poem, commenting on the more mysterious and secretive aspects of Freemasonry:

> *'And therefore what I throw off is ideal -*
> *Lowered, leavened like a history of Freemasons*
> *Which bears the same relation to the real,*
> *As Captain Parry's voyage may do to "Jason's."*
> *The Grand Arcanum's not for men to see all;*
> *My music has some mystic diapasons;*
> *And there is much which could not be appreciated*
> *In any manner by the uninitiated'* [28]

The alliteration of the words '*Lowered*' and '*leavened*' gives an emphasis to the mention of '*a history of Freemasons*', a Masonic metaphor suggesting a transformation of sorts. Byron also refers to the '*uninitiated*', and how they cannot appreciate the mystical secrets of the '*Grand Arcanum*' and thus will never find what was lost.

There is no evidence of Byron being a Freemason, but he was a member of the Italian Carbonari, a Masonic-like secret society which shared similar symbolism though had a radical political ethos. Carbonari means 'makers of charcoal', though like Freemasonry, the secret society was of a speculative nature, and symbolically represented political and social purification, the brethren spreading liberty, morality, and progress. Having left England in 1816, Byron entered into a self-imposed exile to escape the scandalous rumours and mounting debt. It was during his period in Italy that Byron wrote parts of *Don Juan*, the leading character also becoming entwined in secret societies and political and sexual intrigue.

The Carbonari shared similar secret symbolism with Freemasonry, and met in lodges which, like Freemasonry, conducted a ritual. The Carbonari however were linked to militant revolutionaries in Italy who desired a democratic constitution and freedom from Austrian domination, and were the driving force behind the Naples uprising in 1820. Byron, being attracted to the rich political intrigue and the Romantic idea of revolution, was elected 'Capo' of the 'Americani', a branch of the Carbonari in Ravenna, where Byron stayed between 1819 – 1821, buying arms for the cause and meeting with senior members of the conspiracy.[29] Indeed, he writes excitedly of his Carbonari associations on February 18th, 1821:

> '*To-day I have had no communication with my Carbonari cronies: but, in the mean time, my lower apartments are full of their bayonets, fusils, cartridges, and what not. I suppose they consider me as a depot, to be sacrificed, in case*

of accidents. It is no great matter, supposing that Italy could be liberated, who or what is sacrificed, it is a grand object – the very poetry of politics. Only think – a free Italy!!![30]

Another poet linked to the Carbonari was Gabriel Rossetti, whose revolutionary affiliations in Italy forced him into exile in 1821, and much later the Italian general Giuseppe Garibaldi became involved in the society during the early 1830s.[31] After their initial defeats of 1821, the Carbonari played a successful role in the July 1830 Revolution in France, but a subsequent rising in Italy resulted in failure and a government crackdown on the society ensued. By 1848 they had ceased to exist.

Byron subsequently became attracted to the Greek struggle against the Ottomans, and left for Greece in 1823. Taking up a similar role to what he had fulfilled with the Carbonari, Byron generously financing the Greek cause, paying for the so-called 'Byron Brigade' and arming the revolution. Byron found himself having to somewhat navigate the differing factions within the Greek cause, yet he embraced the war of independence wholeheartedly and was prepared to give his fortune in aid of the cause. However, Byron was to die in Greece of fever in April 1824 at the young age of 36. He is considered a National hero to the Greeks.

Newstead Abbey

If one knows where to look when visiting Newstead Abbey, the ancestral home of Byron, one can find Masonic symbolism, for example the guttering is decorated with the Seal of Solomon, although this dates from the occupation of Colonel Thomas Wildman, a Freemason and an old school friend of Byron's from Harrow, who eventually purchased the estate from the cash-strapped poet in 1818. Wildman became Provincial Grand Master for Nottinghamshire, and was a close friend and equerry to the Duke of Sussex, who visited Newstead on several occasions.

Wildman constructed the Sussex Tower at Newstead in honour of the Grand Master, and improved the Chapter House as a private family

Solomon's Seal on the lead drainpipes of Newstead.

Members of the Byron Lodge pictured outside Newstead Abbey in 1923.

chapel. When Wildman died in 1859, the estate was purchased by William Frederick Webb, who had the chapel re-decorated, and in memory of Wildman, Webb had a stained glass window designed with the central Masonic theme of the construction of Solomon's Temple, which may also echo the building work that Wildman undertook at Newstead. Wildman founded the Royal Sussex Lodge in Nottingham in 1829, and there is also a Byron Lodge in the area which celebrates the Masonic links to the poet, his family and Newstead. Masonic services are still held at the chapel by the lodge.

The Masonic symbolism displayed at Newstead, along with the Solomon's Temple scene on display in the stained glass window, would be instantly recognisable to the initiated, the power and status of both the 'Wicked Lord' Byron and Colonel Wildman within Masonic circles being vividly apparent. A parallel to the Masonic themed stained glass windows and Masonic symbolism in the chapel at Tabley House in Cheshire can be seen here, with Lord de Tabley being the Provincial Grand Master of Cheshire during the latter nineteenth century. There is evidence that Masonic services

Stained glass window of the chapel at Newstead revealing the building of Solomon's Temple.

were held in the chapel. Lord de Tabley had a number of lodges named after him in the Cheshire area, including the De Tabley Lodge No. 941.[32]

The majority of English lodges in the eighteenth and early nineteenth centuries, both Antient and Modern, met in taverns and Inns, but for a lodge to be deeply connected to a prominent local aristocrat, it was symbolic of status for that lodge to meet at his residence, providing a much more elitist and private meeting place. The residences of these important Freemasons became a status symbol proudly boasting the owners Masonic beliefs through the display of symbolism and became an erstwhile home to local lodges, lodges which the owners controlled. When fellow Masons visited the Hall, they could recognise the symbolism instantly, and also recognise the Masonic status of the owner. Houses such as Newstead Abbey and Tabley House both celebrated architecture, with the Gothic of Newstead and the classical design of Tabley House, both houses also celebrating Freemasonry, with both aristocratic families becoming central to Freemasonry in their own particular area, serving as Provincial Grand Masters, and all founding their own prestigious lodges. Newstead undoubtedly had a deep historic link to Freemasonry, and the additional feature of being the residence of the Romantic poet Byron would have certainly added to the status of the building especially amongst the more literary Masonic circles, as his reputation as one of Britain's leading poets grew in stature as the nineteenth century progressed.

Conclusion

The poet Byron was certainly aware of Freemasonry and was attracted to the intrigue that certain secret societies offered, becoming a member of the Carbonari in Italy. His links to Masonry are certainly celebrated today with the Byron Lodge No. 4014 which still holds Masonic services in the chapel at Newstead Abbey, a lodge that also celebrates the Grand Mastership of the 'Wicked Lord' and of Colonel Thomas Wildman's Provincial work in Nottinghamshire. Byron's Masonic references in his poetry are few, however the Romantic themes of his verse certainly resound common Masonic themes of the celebration of ancient architecture and the search of what was lost. Perhaps in the end, Byron found his ultimate Romantic zeal in the cause of revolution, the Carbonari providing a society, like Freemasonry, filled with secret symbolism, but unlike Freemasonry, it supplied the poet with the passion of political change and the essence of Romantic revolt and rebellion.

Part 2: Masonic Lodges, Masonic related Societies and their meeting places

Sir Francis Dashwood, The Hell Fire Club and the Caves of West Wycomb

I first researched Sir Francis Dashwood and the Hell-Fire Caves during my PhD work, and thus I wrote about the Masonic connections to the Hell-Fire gatherings in my thesis, which can be seen in my book *The Genesis of Freemasonry*, first published in 2009. Later, I was asked to write an article on the caves by Mike Kearsley, the editor of *The Square* at the time, and the piece was subsequently published in the magazine in March 2014. Mike Kearsley was great to work with, and I published a number of articles with him during his time as editor.

The frontispiece of the first edition of the *Constitutions*, in 1723, engraved by the Freemason John Pine, celebrates the historical meeting in which the Duke of Wharton became Grand Master. This was a powerful image, showing the newly written *Constitutions* being passed to Wharton, by the previous Grand Master, the Duke of Montagu. In the print, Dr John Theophilus Desaguliers is situated to the right, looking on from the side-lines, servant like.

Wharton was a Jacobite Freemason, who, according to various traditions, may also have been the first French Grand Master, in 1728. He became the Grand Master of the new English Premier/Modern Grand Lodge, in 1722, but was subsequently accused of trying to '*capture Freemasonry for the Jacobites*' and was dismissed, in 1723.[33]

Desaguliers had come into direct conflict with Wharton, and the early history of Grand Lodge, as written in later editions of the *Constitutions*, puts Wharton across negatively, inciting him as over ambitious, and reciting an incident, where he was proclaimed Grand Master, without the consent of Grand Lodge. Wharton had proclaimed himself as Grand Master in an irregular lodge, without the proper ceremonials, coming directly into conflict with the Grand Lodge oligarchy who disowned Wharton's authority. It was only through the intervention of the Duke of Montagu, that Wharton was officially accepted as Grand Master.[34]

Wharton was also a political ally of William Cowper, during this period, so he was not without friends within Freemasonry,[35] but his career in the new Grand Lodge ended abruptly on 24th June, 1723, when Lord

Dalkeith was elected Grand Master, stating that '*after some dispute, the Duke of Wharton left the Hall without any ceremony*'.[36]

After his dramatic exit from the Premier/Modern Grand Lodge, Wharton founded the Schemers Club in 1724, which, in keeping with his mischievous nature, was dedicated to the '*advancement of flirtation*'. He had also co-founded the infamous Hell Fire Club, around 1719, which included other Freemasons as participants, such as the Jacobite Earl of Litchfield.

Wharton's untimely death at the age of 33, in 1731, was seen as the ultimate penalty for his excessive indulgence in vice, and his foolish support for the Jacobites. Wharton's close friend Phillip Lloyd, was a member of the Horn Tavern Lodge, and like Wharton, he was a Tory and a member of the Schemers. After Wharton had left England, Lloyd decided to switch his support to Walpole, who subsequently sent him to France to offer Wharton a pardon.[37] Wharton rejected the offer, ultimately becoming the sad epitome of a political genius, seduced by the evil Jacobites.

Wharton's Hell Fire Club came to an abrupt end in 1721, when Walpole's government brought a Proclamation against the '*obscene*' club, swiftly closing it down. They failed to convict anyone for being a member, and imitations of the club subsequently blossomed, notably in Dublin, where a Hell Fire Club, founded by the notorious Richard Parsons, 1st Earl of Rosse, gambled, whored and supposedly dabbled in the occult, until the 1780s.[38] Parsons was also Grand Master of Ireland in 1725.

There was also the infamous club, which Sir Francis Dashwood created, which met at Medmenham Abbey and at West Wycomb, which incidentally was only given the name of the Hell Fire Club long after its demise. Scottish style Hell Fire clubs also appeared, notably the Beggar's Benison Club, which was founded near Fife in 1732 and, like Dashwood's club, only attained notoriety, much later.[39]

Sir Francis Dashwood, Hell Fire, the Masonic Room and West Wycombe

Dashwood became personally involved in the design of his mansion at West Wycombe, which had two Palladian porticos and boasted a number of small temples within the estate. The Hall also had a mysterious 'Masonic Room', which is still a private family room, though, as the name suggests, strong traditions of Masonic-like secret societies were present within the family. However, there are no records which link Dashwood to Freemasonry. Erstwhile members of Dashwood's Hell Fire Club, also known as the Monks of Medmenham, who were Freemasons, include Benjamin Franklin, who was known to have stayed with Dashwood at his mansion at West Wycomb, and John Wilkes, the MP who was exiled due to his libellous essay in No.45 of *The North Briton*.[40]

In the early 1740s, mock processions were organised by opponents of the new Grand Lodge; this 'Mock Masonry' ridiculing the procession to the Grand Feast through London, which was discontinued in April 1745. The 'mock' processions unsurprisingly ended around the same time. One of the instigators of 'Mock Masonry' was the erstwhile poet Paul Whitehead, who was an associate of Hogarth, and also a member of Dashwood's, Hell Fire Club. It has been suggested that Whitehead may have been a Freemason himself who had failed to acquire a much-desired office.[41]

There is no written evidence that has yet come to light, suggesting that the 'Masonic Room' was used for Masonic meetings, but it certainly celebrates the symbolism of Freemasonry, with the 18th century plastered ceiling of the room decorated with prominent Masonic imagery, such as the compasses. This ceiling decoration is very similar to that of the library at Shugborough Hall, in Staffordshire, with the compasses featuring as a prominent symbol there.

Shugborough Hall was owned by Thomas Anson, a friend and associate of Dashwood, both sharing a fascination of the classical architecture of the ancients. Thomas Anson also co-founded the Dillettanti Society and the Divan Club with Dashwood, and introduced the infamous *Shepherds Monument* to his gardens, which, like the monuments around Medmenham and West Wycombe, displayed Classical and Masonic overtones, presenting a 'secret puzzle' in the form of an encrypted Latin code. The Dillettanti Society was established especially for young gentlemen who had been on the Grand Tour, with the aim of studying the architecture and the artifacts of ancient Greece and Rome, Dashwood obviously drawing from his experiences on the Tour.

Dashwood had the famous caves constructed in the 1740s, where he could hold his secret meetings and weekend parties, the labyrinth-

St. Lawrence's Church.

like-caves leading to a chamber called the Inner Temple, which was situated directly beneath the local Church of St. Lawrence. The interior of the church was copied from the Sun Temple at Palmyra, which was built in the third century AD, and a golden ball was placed on top of the tower of the church by Dashwood. A mausoleum was also constructed near the church.

The Mausoleum which is situated above the caves on the hill next to St Lawrence's Church, built in 1765.

The entrance to the caves is dominated by a Gothic folly, imitating a ruined monastery, though two pillars stand above the entrance itself, creating a curious reminder of the Classical influence. Before one reached the Inner Temple, they would have to cross a water channel, which symbolised the River Styx, which was the river that supposedly separated our world from the underworld. Dashwood's caves are also reminiscent of the caverns described by Bacon in his *New Atlantis*, where the investigations of Solomon's House were pursued and secret knowledge was sought. Dashwood's caves may have influenced other folly-like tunnels, such as the tunnels in Liverpool created by Joseph Williamson after the Napoleonic Wars. Williamson's tunnels also have a central 'banqueting hall', and there are local traditions of Williamson using the tunnels to meet his cohorts.

Dashwood's Hell Fire Club had met at the Gothic, Medmenham Abbey, which was a mediaeval structure that had been rebuilt. This rebuilding, had been directed by Dashwood himself, who had classical temples and naked statues erected in the 'pleasure gardens', and had secret caves dug, in a similar fashion to the caves he would construct at West Wycombe. There was a Roman Room, in which hung portraits of famous prostitutes, and two marble pillars were constructed, reminiscent at a glance to the two pillars of Boaz and Jachin, except in this case, the pillars at Medmenham Abbey were adorned with pornographic 'bastard Latin' inscriptions.

The Abbey was the scene of secret sexual and ritualistic enjoyment by the Monks of Medmenham, with prostitutes and local girls, who were dressed as nuns. Dashwood's 'Monks' indulged themselves accordingly.[42] The Hell Fire gatherings finally moved to West Wycombe, supposedly after complaints by the suspicious locals.

These ritualistic parties, set within a landscape that celebrated the divinity of architecture, embodied the celebration of Nature, and the Deistic and enlightened spirit of natural pleasures, reflecting the Roman orgies of antiquity. It seems that radicalism during the 18th century was entwined with a rebellious attitude towards tradition attitudes of morality; the Hell Fire Club, symbolising a fashionable celebration of liberty.

The entrance to the Hell Fire Caves.

Dashwood's gatherings certainly influenced other outrageous clubs to be founded at other country estates, such as the Demoniacks, which met at John Hall Stevenson's Skelton Castle, in Yorkshire, which he renamed *Crazy Castle*, reflecting the antics that the club got up to there.

The practices of the Hell Fire Club and Freemasonry seem poles apart; though at the core of Dashwood's Hell Fire Club was the ethos of liberty, the praise of architecture, and the enlightened vision of the eighteenth century mind. The fact that a small number of the 'Monks' were (or may have been) Freemasons only produces a tentative connection, but the spirit and essence of the various Hell Fire Clubs that were founded in the eighteenth century, give an insight into the fashion to create clubs anywhere and for any reason. Freemasonry certainly formed a part of this 'clubbing' fashion during this period, and was certainly an influence on some of the members.

Woolton Hall, Liverpool

Through my work with the Adult Learning Service in Liverpool, I conducted many local history courses, and some of these courses allowed us to visit many historical sites in the city. A visit to Woolton Hall with a history group brought back memories to when I was a member of a lodge that met there from 2003 – 2006, even though the Hall had deteriorated and was in a much derelict state. This short article was published on my website, along with the photos for my learners to access them.

The abandoned lodge room in Woolton Hall.

Liverpool still has an excellent collection of mansion houses that once housed the wealthy merchants and industrialists of the port, houses such as Allerton Hall, Croxteth Hall, Knowsley Hall, and Woolton Hall. Woolton Hall however, now lies empty and, at the time of writing, derelict, a sad shell of its former self. Hidden inside though, it still reveals beautiful eighteenth century architecture, the fine restoration work of Robert Adam and the lost lodge rooms of local Freemasons. It was originally built in 1704 for the Molyneux family, and redesigned and rebuilt by Robert Adam in 1772 after the Hall was acquired by Nicholas Ashton. Ashton's father had been a financier for Britain's first industrial canal – the Sankey Canal – which was opened in 1757, a waterway that stretched from St. Helens to Widnes, supplying coal to the growing port of Liverpool from the South Lancashire coalfield.

After the Ashton family, a number of other families resided at the Hall, until it became a hotel at the beginning of the twentieth century. It fell into disrepair until local Freemason John Hibbert purchased the Hall in 1980 and it was renovated and used for events, such as weddings. Local

Woolton Hall as it is now.

lodges began to be catered for by the Hall, and the Woolton Group of lodges in Liverpool used the Hall until 2006; the Hall having two lodge rooms, a Chapter Room, various ante-rooms and the lodges having use of the magnificent dining rooms and bar on the ground floor. Lodges such as the now closed Liberty Lodge No. 3888 and Toxteth Lodge No. 1356 once met in the lodge rooms and had their festive board in the dining room.

The Liberty Lodge Bible. The lodge, which met at the Hall, is now closed.

I was a member of Toxteth Lodge for around nine years, and I can vividly remember meeting in the Hall. As soon as you walked in there was a bar on the left hand side. After a drink you could change into your regalia and enter the wood-panelled lodge room. The dining room was an equally fine experience, being surrounded by wood-panelling again and dining on plates decorated with a design of Woolton Hall.

A dining plate used at Festive Boards and functions.

It was John Hibbert, who had been the Tyler of Toxteth Lodge, that allowed me to have a look in the Hall along with a local history group that I managed, and we had exclusive access to the building, which is now closed to the public and up for sale. The lodge rooms are now empty, the dining rooms quiet and abandoned, though the sense of architectural beauty still remains. The old organ sits alone in one empty and decaying lodge room, and amongst the rubbish strewn on the floor old letters from the West Lancashire Province can be found. The old plates that we once dined on lay broken in the cellar. It is hoped the Hall will be sold and restored to its former glory, it is certainly a hidden historical gem of Liverpool and is well worth visiting.

The Tunnels of Joseph Williamson and a Masonic Enigma

Continuing with the Liverpool theme, this article, which was published in *The Square* in December 2013, and was also printed in the newsletter of the Friends of the Williamson's Tunnels, reflected my deep interest in Liverpool local history. I had attended the University of Liverpool, where I defended my PhD in 2008, and had lectured there and also at the University of Hope in Liverpool. It was with my work with the Adult Learning Service in Liverpool however, that brought me into contact with many local history groups and to the Williamson's Tunnels, which I supported over the years and which is now an excellent historical site open to visitors.

The tunnels of Joseph Williamson in Liverpool continue to fascinate and tantalise historians; the similarities to other tunnels and caves in England, such as the Hell Fire caves of West Wycombe, created by Sir Francis Dashwood in the mid eighteenth century, suggest they may have acted as an eccentric folly, and may been used as a secret meeting place for like-minded gentlemen.

Joseph Williamson was a self-made Liverpool businessman; born in Yorkshire in 1769, his family settled in Warrington, and the young Joseph eventually left for Liverpool, where he was apprenticed to a tobacco merchant. He rose through the ranks, married the boss's daughter, and ended up running the business. He began to make connections in Liverpool Society, and became involved in building houses on what was then the edge of the port on Mason Street, near to the present day Edge Hill area of the city. It was underneath these properties, in an abandoned sandstone quarry, that Williamson began constructing his tunnels, sometime around 1816, giving employment to the returning soldiers of the Napoleonic wars. This reflects the origins of the West Wycombe caves; Dashwood employing the local farm workers to dig the caves after a period of drought and failed harvests during the 1740s, in an attempt to combat poverty. Williamson continued to construct the tunnels until his death in

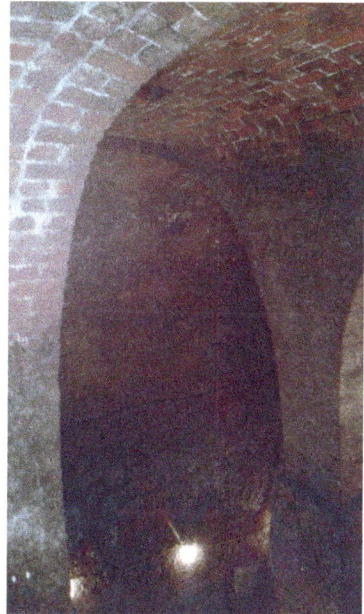

The tunnels of Joseph Williamson.

1840, the labyrinth of tunnels revealing some excellent craftsmanship; with cobbled walkways and brick arches creating a cavernous architectural splendour. Some of the sandstone removed from the tunnels was donated for the building of a local church, and Williamson seemed to convey a philanthropic attitude, which has gained him affection in Liverpool even today.[43]

It has certainly been speculated upon by many of the members of the 'Joseph Williamson Society'[44] and the 'Friends of Williamson's Tunnels'[45] – two groups who take care of different sections of the tunnels, that they may have indeed been used for Masonic meetings; a secret gathering place for like-minded gentlemen, not unlike the Hell Fire Club meetings of the West Wycombe caves, some of the erstwhile members of which, such as MP John Wilkes and American Revolutionary Benjamin Franklin, were known Freemasons.[46]

Caves are still a common meeting place for lodges in various parts of the US, for example, in Kentucky, Masons met in Mammoth Cave. In Oregon, Malheur Cave has been the site of meetings of the Robert Burns Lodge No. 97,[47] and in New Mexico, the Carlsbad Caverns have also witnessed lodge meetings.[48] In Australia, there has also been a lodge, which has met in a cave in New South Wales a number of times. Quarries have also been the location of lodges in both the US and in Australia.[49]

No evidence has yet come to light that Williamson was a Freemason, but there is slight evidence that Freemasons may have been in his tunnels; either digging them or visiting them. Amongst the many common artefacts discovered in the tunnels are clay pipes, and one particular clay pipe bowl was brought to my attention after a visit to the tunnels, one which had the

A clay pipe bowl with a Masonic square and compass on, found in the tunnels.

Masonic symbol of a square and compass on it. Clay pipes were used throughout the eighteenth and nineteenth century, and were fairly common as most men smoked, some were personalised with names and symbols on them; for example anchors and military insignia, and in this case, Masonic symbols.

This particular clay pipe bowl is typical of the ones manufactured in the early nineteenth century; it has the typical ribbed and vine/leaf design, and on the reverse side to the square and compass is a bird, which could be interpreted as a liver bird. So it is possible that the man who smoked this pipe was a Liverpool Freemason. At this time, there were around ten lodges operating in Liverpool, and in 1823, a Masonic rebellion took place in Liverpool which resulted in a separate rebel Grand Lodge operating in the port for a time. There were at least two Liverpool lodges under this Rebel Grand Lodge, but unfortunately, no complete records exists of their members after 1823, even though one of the lodges continued to operate until at least 1858. It is not known where they met after 1823, and their leader, a local engineer and cartographer Michael Alexander Gage was actively involved in local politics, later working against the proposed Liverpool Waterworks Bill in 1850. The liver

A stone jar with a Masonic square and compass on (A trade mark of M. Davies & Son, Manchester) found in the tunnels.

bird was also used as a symbol for some Liverpool based Masonic lodges, such as the Merchants Lodge, a lodge, which supported the rebellion at an early stage, and used the liver bird on its Masonic certificates.[50]

Freemasonry in Liverpool attracted tradesmen, businessmen, professionals, merchants and landowners, so Joseph Williamson and his associates certainly fell into the category of being members of the Craft at that time. Williamson undoubtedly knew the value of local networking; he was a member of the Liverpool Hunt, famously attending the Hunt on his wedding day, and there is the revealing legend of him hosting a dinner for guests in the tunnels; serving, to their disgust, a cheap meal of porridge, which led to a number of the invited gentlemen to leave, only to take his real friends who stayed behind to a magnificent feast in the famed 'banqueting hall'.

Of all Williamson's known associates, none appear to have been members of the Liverpool lodges during the early nineteenth century, though there is one particular name who had a tenuous link to other known Freemasons. Cornelius Henderson painted portraits of a number of prominent Liverpool gentlemen, including William Shepherd, abolitionist and Dissenting Minister of the Gateacre Unitarian Chapel. Shepherd had been taught by none other than the radical Minister Dr Richard Price, a Freemason who was connected to various Dissenting Academies. Price had visited Joseph Priestley while he tutored at the Warrington Dissenting Academy, an Academy, which had a number of tutors that were Freemasons. Shepherd himself had been educated at Holden's Academy near Rainford and at Daventry Academy.[51]

This of course brings us back to the clay pipe bowl with the Masonic symbol of the square and compass; where exactly was it found? What stratified layer of tunnel debris did it come from? The answers to these questions we will never know, and the section of tunnel it was found had been used for dumping the port's refuse during the latter Victorian era. Because of its design, it can be dated to the early part of the nineteenth century – before 1840, and it is likely to have belonged to a local Freemason. The design of the bowl is very similar to pipe bowls found at a clay pipe making 'shop' at the Rookery Farm site, Rainford.[52] There were said to be other clay pipe bowls found with the same Masonic symbol of the square and compass in the tunnels, so there may have been other men in the tunnels from the same lodge, and who knows, one day more concrete evidence may come to light of Masonic activity in the tunnels, with evidence that Williamson himself was a member of the Fraternity.

Lord Leverhulme, Port Sunlight and Freemasonry

Still on the Liverpool theme, I had the pleasure to visit both Port Sunlight on the Wirral and Leverhulme's Liverpool Castle at Rivington Pike with a group of my students on a course I was teaching a few years ago. The Masonic career of Leverhulme was discussed at length during the visits, and this short article was written after the trip with the view of developing it further for a magazine. However, it remained unpublished until now.

The Lady Lever Art Gallery.

William Hesketh Lever – the 1st Viscount Leverhulme (1851-1925) – was an industrialist, philanthropist, Freemason and art collector, whose soap factory and model village for its workers at Port Sunlight, near Birkenhead, Cheshire, became a symbol for the improvement of the living conditions for workers during the latter period of the Industrial Revolution in Britain. Using the themes and ideas of William Morris and the Arts and Crafts Movement, Port Sunlight became a forerunner for the garden suburb, its landscape and architecture creating an aesthetic that, it was thought, would benefit the health and the overall lives of the workers. His philanthropic attitude is reflected in the fact that he was also a keen Mason,

Indeed, Leverhulme was a very active Mason, founding a number of lodges that also conveyed the hierarchy of the workforce at Lever Brothers, and had a number of lodges named after him; the William Hesketh Lever Lodge No. 2916, in which he was initiated into during the lodge's first meeting in 1902, and the Leverhulme Lodge 4438. He also co-founded a number of others and held provincial rank. Today the Lady Lever Art Gallery – famous for its Pre Raphaelite art - situated in Port Sunlight and surrounded by the beautifully rustic-looking workers houses, can be visited for free, and Leverhulme's old

The Masonic chair found in the Lady Lever Art Gallery, once the home of one of Leverhulme's lodges.

lodge room can still be seen in the building, having a number of Masonic items still on display, such as the Masonic chair.

A view of Leverhulme's Liverpool Castle at Rivington Pike.

Leverhulme also had a vision to rebuild Liverpool's lost medieval castle, but he didn't rebuild it in the port, he instead chose Rivington Pike, on the eastern bank of Lower Rivington Reservoir. The original medieval Liverpool castle was built in the fourteenth century, but was demolished in the early eighteenth century as the port was expanding. The 1st Viscount Leverhulme commissioned the construction of this new castle in 1912, but work ceased in 1925 when he died. The castle is thus incomplete and became an extravagant folly, giving an insight into the romantic mind of Viscount Leverhulme.

Freemasonry, the hidden mysteries of nature and science, and the Midlands Enlightenment

The subject matter of this particular article continues the theme of Freemasonry within the Age of Enlightenment, something that I explored during my PhD work, the theme reoccurring in a number of my articles that are included in this book, such as my piece on Edward Jenner. This article was published in *The Square* in June 2014, being another piece for Mike Kearsley.

During the latter half of eighteenth century in an industrial town in the Midlands of England, a number of leading intellectuals and freethinkers met once a month during the time of the full moon to have dinner and discuss natural philosophy. Some Masonic lodges also traditionally met once a month during the time of the full moon so the brethren of the lodge had enough light to find their way home during the otherwise dark streets of an 18th century town in the Winter months. The Warrington based Lodge of Lights passed a resolution in 1810, fixing the regular meeting to *"the Monday Evening on or before the Full Moon"*; the lodge secretary being instructed to make out a list of these Mondays and give them to each member.[53]

Likewise, members of the Royal Lodge of Faith and Friendship, based in Berkeley, Gloucestershire, also proposed that the lodge should meet *"the Monday nearest the Full Moon"*.[54] This is also reminiscent of the Lunar Society, or the Lunar Circle as it was originally called in the mid-1750s, the name given to that group of natural philosophers who met in Birmingham, which included a number of men linked to Freemasonry; boundless intellectuals such as Erasmus Darwin, James Watt, Josiah Wedgwood, Benjamin Franklin and Joseph Priestley. The Lunar Society was thus named, like the aforementioned lodges, because it met on the Monday nearest to the full moon, to provide enough light for the members to travel during the evening.

Though it had a somewhat loose style of membership to say the least, the Lunar Society was an example of like-minded men – or Lunarticks as they styled themselves -working together for a positive aim; to promote natural philosophy. There were no minutes, no constitution and no actual membership list, so only correspondence between 'members' survive to provide an insight into the group. One of the leading 'members' of the society was Erasmus Darwin; a physician, poet and Freemason who was a close friend to many who were linked to the society, such as Josiah Wedgwood and Matthew Boulton.

As the eighteenth century progressed, the idea of immortality became embraced by forward thinking Freemasons, such as Erasmus Darwin, who expressed immortality in his poem The Temple of Nature, discussing modern ideas of immortality with a natural philosophical approach.[55] Darwin studied biology amongst other aspects of natural philosophy, and put forward early ideas of biological evolution in his Zoonomia. In The Botanic Garden, Darwin used Rosicrucian themes of spirits and fairies to symbolise the elements, the older magical images being used to represent new "scientific" thought.

It was this new exploration into natural philosophy and the search for immortality that became an inspiration to Mary Shelley's work Frankenstein. Darwin's theories of artificial production of life and the regeneration of nature, was seen as a direct influence on the gothic classic, giving Mary Shelley a nightmare vision of resurrection and immortality, within the realms of natural philosophy. Another Masonic natural philosopher and friend of Darwin, who has also been linked to the Lunar Society was Benjamin Franklin, who may have also inspired the name of Shelley's masterpiece, Franklin's experiments with lightening rods being an influence.[56]

James Watt was a Scottish inventor and mechanical engineer who had formed a successful partnership with Matthew Boulton, who owned the Soho Manufactory in Birmingham, in 1775. Watt improved the Newcomen steam engine, making the steam engine more efficient, becoming a Fellow of the Royal Society, and also becoming a Freemason.[57] He became an influential member of the Lunar Society, and like Darwin, Wedgwood and Priestley, he became much sought after as an intellectual and conversationalist. When discussing the Lunar Society, one can only imagine the scene of so many leading and important intellectuals sat around a dining table discussing a ground-breaking scientific topic.

Josiah Wedgwood was a close friend of Darwin's, and, though not a Freemason, his name became linked to the Craft. A lodge named after Josiah Wedgwood (No. 2214) was founded in 1887 in Stoke-on-Trent. Josiah Wedgwood's son was a member of the Etruscan Lodge, which met at the Old Bridge Inn at Etruria. Wedgwood's business partner William Greatbatch was also a Freemason and was a member of the Etruscan Lodge.[58] Greatbatch was responsible for designing Masonic artwork on some pottery. This particular Etruscan Lodge closed around 1847, though another lodge with the same name surfaced shortly afterwards. Freemasonry in the Staffordshire area has continued links with the Wedgwood family, and as recently as 1971, two direct descendants of Josiah Wedgwood; with brothers Josiah and William Wedgwood, attending the Josiah Wedgwood Lodge in Stoke.

Another member of the Lunar Society was Joseph Priestley. Priestley was a dissenting minister, philosopher, ground-breaking scientist, a tutor at the non-conformist Warrington Academy, and a supporter of the American and French Revolutions. There is no evidence to suggest that he was a Freemason, but he certainly mixed in Masonic circles. Leading intellectual figures and natural philosophers Dr Richard Price and Benjamin Franklin were both Freemasons, and they both influenced Dr Joseph Priestley in his work while he taught at the Warrington Academy, which, from 1757-1786, became Britain's most progressive learning centre for the sons of non-conformists. Benjamin Franklin is of course, another illustrious name linked to the Lunar Society.

A print of the Warrington Academy, where Dr Joseph Priestley taught.
A son of Josiah Wedgwood attended the Academy.

Creating an intellectual nexus, the Academy became an exceptional and desirable location for students, Priestley expressing its ideology and ethos in his memoirs:

'..the Academy was in a state peculiarly favourable to serious pursuit of truth, as the students were about equally divided upon every question of much importance, such as Liberty and Necessity, the sleep of the soul, and all the articles of theological orthodoxy and heresy ; in consequence of which all these topics were the subject of continual discussion.' [59]

By the mid-eighteenth century, many non-conformist families were involved in industry, such as Josiah Wedgwood, whose son, John, attended the Academy. John 'Iron-Mad' Wilkinson was also a supporter of the Academy, his daughter Mary, marrying Joseph Priestley,[60] and Wilkinson's son, William, also attending the Academy.

Tutors such as Priestley, who became a tutor at the Academy in 1761, and others such as John Reinhold Forster, Dr William Enfield and Jacob Bright, all had excellent reputations, the status of the Academy growing as a result. It was during his time at Warrington that Priestley travelled to London, becoming friends with Benjamin Franklin and Richard Price. The Royal Society would also become an influence on Priestley, when he became a Fellow in 1766 on the merit of his work on electricity. Price and Franklin had both recommended Priestley, and his *History and Present State of Electricity* had been written while he was at Warrington after being encouraged by Franklin to conduct his own experiments.[61] The links between Freemasonry and the Royal Society were still strong at this time, the scientific mind of the eighteenth century being attracted to the expressive ideals of natural philosophy which were apparent in both societies. Priestley finally left the Academy in 1767, and had applied to accompany Captain Cook on his second voyage to the Pacific, but was stopped by the Board of Longitude, which, being mainly made up of the established Anglican Clergy, took offence to Priestley's extreme religious views.

Academy tutor John Reinhold Forster, who had befriended the Freemason Joseph Banks, the botanist who had accompanied Cook on the first voyage, was offered the position on the second voyage instead of Priestley. Forster was one of the two recorded Academy tutors who were Freemasons, being initiated into the Lodge of Lights in Warrington in the same year he came to England, in the December of 1766.[62] Forster later joined the Zu den drei Degan Lodge in Halle, were he worked as a professor of Natural History and Mineralogy after returning from the Cook voyage. He served as orator and warden, though he had to leave the Lodge when he fell into 'adverse circumstances'.[63] His son George, who taught Natural History at Cassel, was also a Freemason, and in 1784, the Zur Wahren Eintracht Lodge in Vienna, held a Lodge of Festivity in honour of his presence there. This Lodge also boasts a variety of other prominent figures of the time, such as Haydn, Alxinger, Denis, Born, Eckhel, and Sonnenfels.[64] Jacob Bright was the second recorded Academy tutor to have been a member of the

Lodge of Lights, entering the lodge some five months before Forster in the July of 1766.[65] Bright played quite an active part in the lodge, becoming Worshipful Master in 1771-2.[66]

Priestley had moved to Birmingham in 1780, and though he had been involved in the society for over a decade, his closer proximity to the 'Lunarticks' resulted in its most productive and prolific phase (it was at this time that the society began to meet on Mondays rather than the usual Sundays to accommodate Priestley's ministerial duties). However, with the advent of the French Revolution in 1789 and the subsequent Priestley Riots in 1791, the society began to suffer; unlike Freemasonry which does not discuss politics in the lodge room, tension between members due to political differences began to fragment the society. Priestley left for the USA in 1794, and Matthew Boulton and James Watt had to arm their employees to protect their Soho Manufactory from rioters. Despite the society being continued by the sons of Wedgwood, Boulton and Watt, it had ceased to exist by 1813, thus one the world's most intellectual and forward thinking collectives came to an end.

Lodges that meet outside and in Caves and Quarries

This article started life in two separate parts; one part can be found in my book *A Quick to Freemasonry*, which was first published in 2013, where I discussed lodges that met outside and in quarries in the US and in Australia. The second part originated as a post on my website, which discussed a lodge meeting in Solomon's Quarries in Jerusalem. I was approached by an editor of *California Freemason Magazine* to compose an article using both pieces, the article being published in the July/August 2019 issue.

In certain rural areas in the United States, there are Masonic lodges that meet on ranches, hilltops, in caves, and in other outside areas, and actually confer degrees and conduct ceremonies. As we shall see, there are many reasons why these lodges meet outside under the open canopy of heaven, or deep within quarries or caves. Some lodges, like the Rose Bride Lodge of Wigan in England, which met in the mid nineteenth century, had lost their lodgings above a pub and were forced to meet outside, others, such as a lodge that still meets in Solomon's Quarries, captures the full essence of Freemasonry, as the lodge celebrates the very location where the stone for the Temple originated. Some outside meetings have become traditional for certain lodges, such as the Castle Lodge No. 122, in Eagle, Colorado, which meets outside on a private ranch annually during the summer.[67] There is also a lodge in Montana, which still meets outside and has Tyler's mounted on horseback, with custom-made aprons for the horses. Of course for a lodge to meet outside, the weather has to be good, and therefore the brethren can open a lodge amidst Nature itself; a perfect setting for a lodge that is meant to represent God's universe. Indeed, for a lodge to meet outside is be surrounded by God's creation, in short, to be surrounded by the work of God himself.

There are many traditional outside meeting places for Masonic lodges in the US; one of the more famous examples being Independence Rock, in central Wyoming, which was a landmark and way-station on the old Oregon Trail, and became the first meeting place for Freemasons in what was to become the State of Wyoming. A similar site exists in Montana at the summit of Mullan Pass, which was the first recorded meeting place of Freemasons in the State in 1862. A stone alter and stone Officer's stations have been erected there.[68] In Indiana, a rock quarry was used as a meeting place for eighteen hundred Masons in 1967, using forty-five Tylers positioned around the rim of the quarry, and at a quarry in Marietta,

Ohio, Tylers on horseback shouted from the rim of the quarry to report. Caves are also a common meeting place for lodges in the US, for example, in Kentucky, Masons met in Mammoth Cave, in Oregon, Malheur Cave has been the site of meetings of the Robert Burns Lodge No. 97,[69] and in New Mexico the Carlsbad Caverns have also witnessed lodge meetings.[70]

Caves do appear in certain degrees found within Richard Carlile's *Manual of Freemasonry*, which was first published in England as an exposé in Carlile's radical journal *The Republican* in 1825, such as the Degree of Scotch Master, which mentions a cave near Aberdeen in Scotland, where Masonry had been preserved by its inhabitants.[71] Another degree in Carlile's *Manual* that mentions a cave is the Degree of Nine Elected Knights, where an assassin of Hiram Abiff takes refuge. This is a degree that is also reminiscent of the Elu of Nine Degree in the Ancient and Accepted Scottish Rite.[72] The mention of the cave is interesting as it reminds us of Plato's *Allegory of the Cave* and its underlying theme of man escaping the primitive darkness of the cave and being born into the light, which has stark Masonic parallels, and can be seen especially with the First Degree initiation ceremony, and also reflects how the Mason continues to tread the enlightened pathway of the further degrees.[73]

In England, for a lodge to meet outside is now unheard of, but there was a lodge under the Grand Lodge of Wigan during the mid-nineteenth century, that did meet under a bridge by the Leeds and Liverpool Canal near Wigan, in the north-west of England. This particular lodge called the Rose Bridge Lodge, was quite short lived, but was an interesting reminder that lodges could once meet this way. Apparently the lodge posted a Tyler at either end of the canal towpath to keep out intruders.[74] Meeting outside, under the sun, the moon and the stars, is for a lodge to meet under the active, natural Universe itself, and as long as the weather is good, there would be no place better. Lodges have also been known to meet outside in India, and in Australia, one New South Wales lodge has met a couple of times in a large cave, and there is a Mark Lodge, which has met in a quarry in Australia. The quarry in question had supplied the stone for the Grand Lodge building in Brisbane.

A few years ago, I was contacted by a good friend and Brother George Shukha, from a lodge in Israel, who informed me about a lodge meeting in Solomon's Quarries, a rather famous cave in Jerusalem, very well known in Masonic circles. The photos of the event were captivating, and the meeting included a lecture by Brother Yosef Bahar. Solomon's Quarries – known as

Photos by George Shukha.

Zedekiah's Cave – is situated under the Muslim Quarter of the Old City of Jerusalem, and is believed to have been the quarries that supplied the stone for the Temple. Cherub graffiti was found in the cave by a nineteenth century French archaeologist, which has been used to support that the quarries were used in Solomon's time, and Masonic lodges have met in the cave since the later nineteenth century.

As Brother Bahar explained 'It all started when brethren from "Cukurova Lodge" in Adana (a city in the south-eastern part of Turkey) invited me on March 2015, to give a lecture on Zedekiah's Cave – King Solomon's Quarries. I gave the lecture, the brethren liked it and were very interested to visit Jerusalem and have a lodge meeting in the cave. So our "Nur Lodge" in Tel-Aviv (it is a Turkish speaking-working lodge) made all the preparations and logistics and on the 7th of September 2015, and we had a working in the cave. Thirty two brethren from Nur Lodge and 130 visiting Brethren from Turkey — including the Grand Masters—participated on that lodge meeting. They asked me to repeat my lecture for the brethren who did not hear it (there were brothers from Istanbul and Izmir). The lecture was in Turkish and a Hebrew translation printed for the Israeli brethren. Attached are pictures of the cave prepared for that occasion.' A recent meeting in the cave took place on the 12th of March this year, with Freemasons from the US, Germany, Romania, Cyprus and Turkey, attending the event.

The cave has indeed been an important feature in Freemasonry during its long history, from certain lodges meeting in caves, to the cave itself having an underlying philosophical background within the Masonic ritual. Like lodges that meet outside under the canopy of the heavens, a lodge that meets in a cave is utilising nature, a natural lodge room that reflects the fundamental initiatory aspects of Freemasonry itself, especially reflected in the parallels of Plato's *Allegory of the Cave*, the initiate being reborn from primeval darkness into light. Working a lodge in the natural setting of God's universe is indeed utilising the essence of Nature to praise Nature, and thus both meeting in a cave and outside is a perfect setting for a lodge.

Part 3: Revolution and Rebellion

Thomas Paine, Freemason?

This article is another example of the reoccurring theme of Freemasonry during the Age of Enlightenment within my work, and this particular section of the book examines the more political actions of Freemasons during this period of the late eighteenth and early nineteenth centuries. These political actions, such as the American War of Independence and the French Revolution, being events that occurred in the wake of the Enlightenment. This particular article on Thomas Paine, which kicks off this section, appeared in *Freemasonry Today* in the autumn 2008 issue.

> *I know, however, but of one ancient book that authoritatively challenges universal consent and belief, and that is Euclid's Elements of Geometry...*
> Thomas Paine, *The Age of Reason, Part II, Chapter 1,* 1795.

Thomas Paine is celebrated today as an eighteenth century revolutionary, radical and republican who wrote countless controversial but ground breaking pamphlets, such as *Common Sense* and *The Age of Reason*. He also wrote the enigmatic *Origins of Freemasonry*, published posthumously as part ritual exposé and part Masonic pseudo-history. His interests in Freemasonry were obvious, and the fact that some of his supporters and associates, such as Benjamin Franklin, George Washington, James Monroe, La Fayette, Nicolas de Bonneville and Richard Price, were Freemasons, has led some historians, such as Margaret Jacob, to believe Paine was also a Mason.[75] Certainly during the nineteenth century, Masonic historians such as R.F. Gould and A.F.A. Woodford went to painstaking lengths to distance Paine from the Craft, his very association to Freemasonry causing embarrassment and shame, with Gould even stating that Paine wasn't the author of the exposé. Woodford dismissed Paine's involvement with Freemasonry, declaring that his exposé had no value, and contemptuously stated that Masonry was no way honoured with Paine's connection, not wanting the Craft to be associated with such a political radical. Ironically, all of the attention that Paine received from Masonic historians was seen as proof in itself in some circles.[76]

Paine's colourful life began in Thetford in 1737. He was set to follow his Quaker father as a corset-maker, but he was never at rest and constantly sought knowledge. His first wife died in childbirth, and Paine seemed to enter a period where he did various jobs, drifting into teaching and finally working in excise. He married for a second time, though they were to separate as Paine's interest in politics developed. His first foray into the political arena was to petition Parliament on behalf of his fellow excisemen for better working conditions, an adventure which led him to the London coffee-houses and to a meeting with Freemason Benjamin Franklin, who was visiting London at the time. Paine's lobbying was ignored and he lost his job as a result, so in 1774, on invitation from Franklin himself, he left for the American colonies.

Once there, Paine settled into Philadelphia and with an introduction from Franklin, he became the editor of the Pennsylvania Magazine, quickly becoming a man of letters, embracing the spirit of political reform in America. Indeed, Franklin was constantly name-dropped into his writings, Paine using him as a seal of approval. It was his use of 'common' language, so easily understood by the America people, which made his pamphlet *Common Sense* so successful during the American Revolution, gaining Paine the admiration and support of another Freemason, George Washington. Paine's writing skills and friendship with Franklin and Washington enabled him to stay at the forefront of the political action and he was made secretary to Congress' Committee for Foreign Affairs from 1777-79. After Paine left the position, he continued to be active in foreign affairs, and letters from Paine to Washington reveal a personal friendship at this time, Washington arranging a hefty salary for Paine. Despite this, Paine was not happy at the way the Revolution was going with the political power being shared by the landowning elite, and he began to make enemies.[77]

In 1787, Paine returned to England, were he once again entered into political debate, joining radical clubs in London with William Blake (no stranger to Freemasonry himself) and promoted his invention of an iron bridge. When the French Revolution erupted in 1789, Paine saw an opportunity to start again and wrote *The Rights of Man* in response to Edmund Burke's rebuke of the Revolution. Burke had written in answer to Richard Price's sermon on the Revolution, and Paine defended the Freemason Price, confirming the natural rights of man against the tyranny of Kings, supporting the ideas of the Enlightenment made popular in France by Voltaire. Paine fled for France on the advice of Blake, and again with the help of friends like the Freemason La Fayette, he entered the political arena, assisting in forging the new French Constitution.[78]

However, events soon turned sour with the Terror, and as an Englishman who spoke no French, he began to attract suspicion and gained enemies after pleading for the life of King Louis. He was imprisoned, and only released by the intervention of another Freemason, James Monroe in 1793. However, it was not all harmony with his old American revolutionary friends; he attacked Washington in a published letter in 1796, a letter that did not win him any support. Paine stayed on in France living for a time with Monroe and another Freemason Nicolas de Bonneville, where he completed his most controversial work to date: *The Age of Reason*. Spiritually, Paine supported the approach known as Deism – a belief system which derives the existence of God based on Reason as opposed to sacred scripture, and in *The Age of Reason*, Paine refers to God in a scientific sense as a Creator of a mechanized Universe. Disillusioned, he finally departed to the USA in 1802 with the help of Thomas Jefferson, who had also moved in a Masonic milieu, although actual proof of his membership has never been found. Paine died seven years later, an outcast with only six mourners attending his funeral.

Paine sought a Utopian vision for the world, embracing the recognizable essence of Freemasonry, promoting ideals such as democracy, education, morality, religious toleration, and the fashionable Newtonian natural philosophy, Paine sharing Newton's views that the existence of God was to be found in Nature. Indeed, in part one of his *Age of Reason*, a number of chapters are dedicated to the Newtonian system of the Universe, in a fashion which is very similar to the presentation of the Craft ritual, giving an almost poetical description of the Earth and five other planets rotating around the Sun, explaining how gravity orders the harmony of the Solar system. The search for the hidden mysteries of Nature and Science certainly captivated Paine who himself dabbled in architecture and experimented with inventions, designing an iron bridge and a smokeless candle.[79]

His *Origins of Free-Masonry*, which was regarded after his death as a missing chapter belonging to the unpublished third part of the *Age of Reason*, presented a description of the Masonic ritual along with his theory that Freemasonry was a form of Sun worship. Curiously, the essay fits in with his work in the *Age of Reason*, and as a whole it follows a mystical Newtonian theme of a modern ordered Universe that complements God as being revealed in Nature and Reason. The work certainly echoes Masonic themes, with Paine using ancient knowledge by Euclid to support his views on the Newtonian Universe and discussing the Biblical cubit, a measurement used in the construction of Solomon's Temple.[80]

Paine did however make a lasting contribution to Freemasonry, his *Origins* being highly influential to Richard Carlile's *Manual of Freemasonry*, Carlile quoting Paine when writing his thoughts on the Craft's history. A number of lodges in the USA were also named after Paine, and when he died many lodges throughout America honoured him. If Paine did enter into Freemasonry, it would have been during the period of the American Revolution, his life being at the epicentre of the social elite at that time, his closeness in that era to the likes of Franklin, Washington, La Fayette and Monroe suggesting that he was undoubtedly aware of their Masonic membership. Paine was certainly attracted to clubs and societies throughout his life, such as the White Hart Club, which Paine attended when he was an exciseman in Lewes.[81] He was also involved with the Theophilanthropists and the Philosophical Society, in which he discussed the Newtonian Universe and Euclid's geometry.[82] Paine was unquestionably informed by the ethos of Freemasonry, an ethos that influenced his writings and inspired his vision of a just and fairer society, an aspiration wholly in accord with Freemasonry today as much as in the later eighteenth century. What was dangerously revolutionary and radical then, is much applauded now.

The Grand Lodge of Stockport

This article appeared in *The Square* in March 2015. The Grand Lodge of Stockport was a little-known-about independent Masonic body that was mentioned in the minutes of the Lodge of Sincerity, the leading lodge of the Grand Lodge of Wigan, in the nineteenth century, and I was able to piece together enough information to write an entertaining short article for the magazine. I'm still awaiting that magical find that could reveal more about this mysterious Grand Lodge....

The Liverpool Masonic Rebellion and its subsequent formation as the Wigan Grand Lodge is perhaps the most well-known example of organised discontent amongst Freemasons in the wake of the 1813 union of the 'Moderns' and 'Antients' in England. However, there was a brief mention of another 'rebel' body of Masons in the industrial north-west of England during the late 1830s; the mysterious Grand Lodge of Stockport. Its mention occurs in the now lost minute book of the Lodge of Sincerity – the leading Wigan lodge attached to the Wigan Grand Lodge, which, for a period during 1837, referred to correspondence between the lodge and the Grand Lodge of Stockport, discussing a possible union between them. Nothing came of the idea, and the Grand Lodge of Stockport disappeared into the dense smog of early Victorian history, forever to be lost.[83]

However, the correspondence discussed that the Grand Lodge of Stockport was expanding at the time, that it had a Grand Master named Ruben Hopwood, and had opened a new lodge in Manchester called the St. Alban's Lodge, and was about to open three more lodges. The leading lodge was named St. John's Lodge, and both Grand Lodges appeared to share the same independent ethos of Freemasonry.

The reference to the Grand Lodge of Stockport in the now lost minutes of the Lodge of Sincerity was first published in a paper by the renowned Masonic historian Norman Rogers, who obtained the minute book along with other documents from Sincerity during the late 1940s. According to the last secretary of the lodge who I got to know during my research for my recent book on the Wigan Grand Lodge, the old minute books were never given back and became lost after Rogers' death.[84]

There is no other trace of the Grand Lodge of Stockport, but I have found a likely contender for its Grand Master Ruben Hopwood. Ruben, sometimes spelled Reuben or Rueben in various records, was a shoe maker in Stockport, born c.1792, and resided in the Hillgate area of the town. He was baptised in the Presbyterian Church in Stockport in 1792, attended Sunday School, he married Mary Gooch in 1812, and had a number of children, including a son who was also called Reuben, born in 1821. Like his father, he was also a shoe maker, and his son; John William Hopwood, carried on the family tradition and worked as a shoe maker in Stockport throughout the rest of the nineteenth century.[85]

The members of the Liverpool Masonic rebellion and the subsequent Wigan Grand Lodge also had similar 'high street' trades; watchmakers, tailors, jewellers, gunsmiths, and if this Rueben Hopwood is the same as the Grand Master mentioned in the correspondence, then he certainly shared a similar background with his Wigan and Liverpool brethren.

The next mention of the Wigan Grand Lodge being in touch with Freemasons from that area is to be found in 1843, when a deputation was sent to meet and observe brethren from the '*St. John's and St. Paul's Societies*' in Ashton-under-Lyne, which was another industrial cotton producing town situated not too far from Stockport. Brethren from these '*Societies*' were brought into the Wigan fold and formed the St. Paul's Lodge No. 6 under the Wigan Grand Lodge.[86] Could these '*Societies*' have been the remnants of the Grand Lodge of Stockport? There is no direct evidence, but it is strange that a group of brethren from what appears to be two lodges from that area – east of Manchester, and not connected to the United Grand Lodge of England, had made contact with the Wigan Grand Lodge. Of the members of St. Paul's Lodge, we know of only a few; John Glover was a publican who ran the Concert and Theatre Tavern in Ashton-under-Lyne, and Isaac Kirk.[87] They both served as Officers in the Wigan Grand Lodge, though nothing is heard of the St. Paul's Lodge after 1848.

So, are there long lost minute books relating to the Grand Lodge of Stockport hidden away on some dusty shelf somewhere in Stockport? Or could the correspondence to the Lodge of Sincerity in 1837 have been a hoax? Certain documents that Norman Rogers had taken for his research have turned up; copies of the membership lists of the Lodge of Sincerity have been returned and correspond perfectly with what Rogers transcribed in his paper, and members of Sincerity today are still very much aware of missing minute books that were taken at the time by Rogers, which point to Rogers' transcription of actual documents being wholly credible. Also, the fact that a Ruben or Rueben Hopwood existed in Stockport at the time supports that the correspondence was contemporary and was based on some truth. So, until an old minute book is discovered in some dark archives of Stockport, we will have to continue to ponder the mystery of the Grand Lodge of Stockport.

Secrecy and Suppression: Freemasonry and the Unlawful Society Act

This article was the first in a series of articles commissioned by Michael Baigent for *Freemasonry Today*, where it was published in spring 2008, which examined the radical and social aspects of Masonry in England during the late eighteenth and early nineteenth centuries. Baigent always requested no footnotes for the articles, so I have attempted to place some in this piece to act as references for source material and further reading where needed.

The closing years of the eighteenth century were enveloped in a climate of fear, with the Tory government of William Pitt the younger suffering the anxiety of revolution, rebellion and riot. The French Revolution in 1789, the subsequent Bloody Terror and the rise of Napoleon had cast a shadow of dread over Great Britain. This had been compounded by rebellion in Ireland in 1798 and frequent riots and protests by the working classes, with groups of factory workers combining to form seemingly ever more aggressive 'trade unions'. Radical societies such as the 'United Irishmen' and the 'London Corresponding Society' were singled out as extremist and treasonous.[88]

The alarm of secret gatherings of men swearing oaths to solidify their united cause created a powerful image of the haunting spectre of Jacobinism, and Freemasonry, both 'Antient' and 'Modern', was to be associated with these societies in the over fretful minds of the government. When the Unlawful Societies Act was passed in July 1799, Freemasonry was unavoidably affected, the Craft having to adapt to what many saw as an oppressive legislation. The original proposal of the bill would have completely banned Freemasonry along with other secret societies, but the Earl of Moira and other leading Freemasons from both the 'Moderns', the 'Antients' and the Scottish Grand Lodge prevailed upon Pitt to amend it by exempting Masonic lodges *'sitting by the precise authorization of a Grand Lodge and under its direct superintendence'*. This however would have destroyed the unattached Scottish lodges like Lodge Kilwinning and so the latter, aided by their Scottish MP William Fullerton who knew Pitt, obtained a further alteration on behalf of the lodge. The bill in its final form stated that exempt from its provisions were *'all Lodges declaring upon oath before a Justice of the Peace that they were Freemasons'*.[89]

Thus Freemasonry managed to escape the Act by agreeing to submit annual returns of lists of members and lodge meetings which could be inspected by the appropriate authorities. Masonry would henceforth have an element of transparency, but did Freemasons in general feel comfortable with this new declaration? And how did the general public feel about Freemasonry during this atmosphere of political anxiety? Answers to these questions can be found at local level, were the individual lodges showed signs of change and transition, especially in the industrial heartland of England were radicalism amongst the working classes was most associated.

For example, the 'Modern' Lodge of Lights, based in the industrial town of Warrington in the north-west of England, mentioned in its minutes of August 1799, that, in accordance to the recent Act, it would hereafter submit a list of its members every March. The lodge underwent a further transition, reflected in the occupations of the new members. It became diluted with more working class members, its membership lists filled with a healthy mix of weavers, tin plate workers, painters, plasterers and fustian cutters, occupations which were few and far between before 1799. These working men appeared to fill the gap left by a high percentage of gentlemen and professional classes who seemed to distance themselves from the lodge during this sensitive period.[90]

The lodge minutes also reflect this concern during the first few decades of the nineteenth century and efforts were made to regain the membership of the local gentry. For example, in the January of 1800, the Secretary of the lodge wrote, '*I think there is a prospect of the Lodge being once more respectable as several Gentlemen have expressed their desire to become members.*' Two prominent gentlemen, James and Charles Turner, did join in the October of that year, James being a Lieutenant in the Lancashire Militia, Charles being a cotton manufacturer, bringing hopes that suspicions about the nature of the lodge could be dispelled.[91]

These suspicions were very real in Warrington at this time, for example, in 1802, during the funeral for Brother John Johnson, the minutes record '*It was asserted that the spectacle removed from the greater part of the onlookers and the public those prejudices which have so much prevailed against the Order especially in this place.*' Despite this attempt at winning local hearts and minds, the local people were suspicious of the lodge, and a notable low attendance rate is evident at this time. In 1806, the average attendance was only six to nine members, and by 1808, the membership was reduced to seven. In January and February of 1809, only four members were present, and by March, there was a desperately low turnout of three. The Lodge of Light had entered a rocky period after the Unlawful Society Act, and it took a number of decades to recover.[92]

Another lodge which suffered from low attendance during this period was the Oldham based Lodge of Friendship, which, like the Lodge of Lights, was a 'Modern' lodge, and had a notable influx of working men joining, again replacing gentlemen who had distanced themselves from Freemasonry, especially in Industrial towns in the north-west of England. Further evidence for working men joining Freemasonry also appears in a lodge in Nantwich, which had the rather loyal name of the King's Friends Lodge. The lodge was constituted in Chester in 1793, and in 1808, it was noted in the minutes that a large number of the brethren of the lodge were of a more working class standing, with members having occupations such as locksmith, haymaker, ropemaker and skinner.[93]

Certainly in some industrial towns during the sensitive years after the Unlawful Societies Act, the local gentlemen distanced themselves, and in their absence working men filled the lodges. Indeed, the immediate years following the Act saw fewer 'Modern' lodges being founded and the 'Antient' lodges re-using existing numbers of lodges which had become defunct rather than issue new warrants. This was a result of the 'Antients' having imposed emergency measures on themselves after their meeting with Pitt, stating that they would '*suppress and suspend all masonic meetings, except upon the regular stated lodge meetings*', a declaration which enforced that only their current lodges at the time of the bill would operate, the Grand Lodge refusing to issue new warrants. The 'Antients' may have done this because of their close relationship with Irish Freemasonry, or perhaps because of the large number of lodges under their jurisdiction within the industrial north-west of England.

Because Freemasonry adapted in response to the threat of the Unlawful Societies Act, it survived and eventually became stronger. The Painite radical Richard Carlile writing in his *Manual of Freemasonry* said of the Act that '*the legislature being about to deal with other secret societies, would do well now not again to make an exception of Masonry*', Carlile realising that the Craft had escaped a possible period of persecution.[94] Freemasonry's survival testifies that the knee-jerk reaction of politicians can be misjudged and flawed. The Revolutionary Freemason de La Fayette when commemorating the fall of the Bastille, once said: '*May this great monument, raised to Liberty, serve as a lesson to the oppressor, and an example to the oppressed*', a quote which could as easily refer to Freemasonry in relation to the Act which, if not for rigorous political negotiation and adaptability, may not have survived the repressive political action of 1799.

The American Revolution, Freemasonry and the Trans-Atlantic connection

This article was yet another commissioned by Michael Baigent for *Freemasonry Today*, where it was published in spring, 2010. The theme of revolution, rebellion and Freemasonry seemed to be quite popular, and I was asked for similar work in the same vein.

American Freemasonry had been established as early as the 1720s, and one of the most important centres for the Craft in the new colonies was Boston, a port which played a major role in the development of Masonry. In 1733, the famous St. John's Lodge was constituted at the Bunch of Grapes Tavern in Boston, a lodge which, over the years had been attended by such famous Freemasons as George Washington, Benjamin Franklin, La Fayette, James Otis and John Rowe, all men who played a role in the Revolution. Boston was the busiest port in the Massachusetts Bay Colony and had a link to all the major ports in Britain, especially Liverpool and Glasgow, trading in all manner of products, exporting merchandise such as tobacco and rum, and importing goods such as tea.

Because of the extensive trade, Boston was visited by countless merchants, seeking new business contacts and networking, establishing Trans-Atlantic relationships which would remain strong even in times of conflict. Freemasonry definitely played a part in this networking, the lodge lists of Boston revealing at the time an array of visiting Freemasons. Likewise a glance at the Liverpool lodges from the same period shows a similar list of visiting merchants from America. For example, visiting the Liverpool Merchants Lodge in 1789 is a merchant named Melling Wolley, whose residence is given as New Orleans, and another, John Samuel Thompson, is listed as a merchant from Santa Cruz . Other Liverpool lodges, such as the Antient Union Lodge, also list a number of merchants and mariners visiting from as far away as New York, Boston and Bermuda during this period, testifying to the intricate Masonic links between Trans-Atlantic ports and the networking that could be offered.[95]

There are certainly distinct parallels between the Liverpool based Merchants Lodge and the St. Andrew's Lodge in Boston, both having a high percentage of young, well connected and powerful merchants as members, intent on gaining a hold on local politics. Indeed, the Merchants Lodge included such significant local gentlemen as Thomas Golightly, Thomas Barton and William Ewart, all having interests in shipping and local politics.[96] The St. Andrew's Lodge, which met at the infamous Green Dragon Tavern in Boston, has attracted many legends regarding the Boston Tea Party, which took place on the 16th of December 1773 and was the pivotal event which kick-started the American Revolution. The lodge, which has been connected to the planning of the Tea Party, which resulted in men dressed as Indians boarding a British vessel and throwing the over taxed tea overboard, included amongst its members the likes of John

Paul Revere
(Grand Lodge of Massachusetts)

Hancock, Dr Joseph Warren and Paul Revere, again all local leaders of the community who played a role in the Revolution.

Another lodge which has attracted study in recent years was the Virginia based Fredericksburg Lodge, which had included members from numerous countries during the latter eighteenth century, including Scottish merchants from Glasgow, which like Liverpool was a thriving industrial port. Scottish Freemasons in the locality included Robert Bogle who represented his father's Glasgow firm in Port Royal and the American Revolutionary naval hero John Paul Jones. Freemasonry became vital for the social networking of young merchants and settlers, the Craft allowing them to make new contacts in the area and to form a bond with like-minded men. Other Scottish members of the Fredericksburg Lodge included Walter Stewart, Andrew Beaty and James Hunter. Hunter was a Scottish émigré who became an extremely successful merchant, his brother Adam negotiating trade contracts with their Scottish relatives while James took care of the business in Virginia, buying goods for sale in Britain. Other prominent Freemasons associated with Fredericksburg were George Washington and James Monroe.

The American Revolution caused economic and social upheaval for the colonies, and the fact that so many Freemasons took part in the Revolution resulted in members of the same lodge fighting on different sides. An example of this can be seen with the St. Andrew's Lodge with Dr

Joseph Warren fighting for the Americans, while another member of the same lodge, Dr John Jeffries, fought for the British. Politics seems to have permeated into American Freemasonry, and with loyalties divided, some Freemasons found their fellow brethren hostile, such as Boston Mason John Rowe who tried to remain neutral, only to be openly insulted by his fellow brethren.

The Masonic historian Steven Bullock has discussed how loyalties were divided in America between the Antients, who, he states, were on the whole supporters of the Revolution, and the Moderns, who appeared to be Loyalists. The St. Andrew's Lodge was an Antient lodge, though the lodge still had brethren fighting for the British, such as the aforementioned John Jeffries. Compared to the Antients, the Moderns did suffer during the war, though this may be explained due to the easiness of Antient lodges to establish traveling Warrants, whereas the Moderns had to suspend meetings during the conflict. After Independence was gained, the Masonic problem then arose of also being independent or remaining loyal to the respective Grand Lodge, as both Antient and Modern were British. In this respect, American Freemasonry witnessed a further political dilemma, and though the idea of a national American grand lodge was put forward, the future lay in state organized grand lodges. Visiting Freemasons could still attend lodges on either side of the Atlantic, the Liverpool lodges for example, both Antient and Modern, being filled with visiting merchants and sailors from all over America.

The American Revolution certainly affected American Freemasonry, dividing loyalties, not only politically but in the altering of the structure and organization of the American Craft. Despite the upheavals, Freemasonry undoubtedly assisted in healing the divisions, especially locally, the evidence for which can be clearly seen in the lists of visiting Masons attending lodges from both sides of the Atlantic. Liverpool lodges from the 1780's onwards are filled with visiting American merchants and sailors, and similarly Boston and Virginian lodge lists reveal British merchants and sailors. Freemasonry positively supported the continuation and development of Trans-Atlantic trade links, merchants, seamen and settlers finding familiar and recognizable surroundings in a lodge while being thousands of miles from home.

Freemasonry and the French Revolution

When I read articles by other Masonic writers, I tend to like the style of writing that is straight to the point and easy to understand. With that in mind, I wrote this article on Freemasonry and the French Revolution, condensing the important information into an average size article. The piece was commissioned by Michael Baigent and published in *Freemasonry Today* in summer 2009. At his request there was no footnotes, although I have added some books related to this subject in the bibliography.

It seems that during the Eighteenth Century, whenever there was a Revolution, Freemasons were not far away. The American Revolution had many Masons leading the cause, such as Benjamin Franklin, George Washington and John Hancock to name but a few, and with the outbreak of the French Revolution in 1789, Freemasons were again involved in the leadership of various factions, with Louis Philippe II, Duke of Orleans, the Grand Master of the Grand Orient being prominent, along with the Marquis de Lafayette and Jean Paul Marat. As with the American Revolution, Freemasons were divided, their differing views and loyalties challenging not only the course of the Revolution, but the perception of Freemasonry in France and around the globe.

Masonic symbolism also featured prominently in Revolutionary propaganda and in official pamphlets for the Revolutionary governments, symbols such as the All Seeing Eye and the Plumb-Rule being used to portray the supposed Enlightenment and justice brought about by the Revolution. The Enlightenment itself, brought to prominence by writers like the Freemason Voltaire, had an engaging influence on the origins of the Revolution, with works such as *The Rights of Man* by Thomas Paine, who had also been linked to many Freemasons, being written in support of the Revolution. The Revolution however, descended into violence and political turmoil, the enlightened road of liberty being a long and blood stained one, with an estimated 15,000-40,000 people being guillotined. The guillotine was named after Dr Joseph-Ignace Guillotine, physician, Assembly member and Freemason.

Louis Philippe II, Duke of Orleans

The Grand Master of the Grand Orient de France, Louis Philippe II, Duke of Orleans was an anglophile who visited England frequently. He was friends with the Prince of Wales, who had also served as Grand Master for a time for the English based 'Modern' Grand Lodge. Louis Philippe held and promoted liberal views and was despised by Marie Antoinette, the royal court being suspicious that he was after the throne himself. French politics was in desperate need of reform, the Estates-General being the representative assembly consisting of three estates, the First Estate being the clergy, the Second Estate consisting of the nobility and the larger Third Estate being the common people (landowners, merchants and professionals). Agitation within the Third Estate mounted in 1789 with a group of liberals demanding change. At this time Louis Philippe was involved in the Second Estate at the head of the liberal minority. He subsequently led a small group of noblemen to join the Third Estate, which declared itself the National Assembly in June 1789.

The Marquis de Lafayette was also a nobleman who left the Second Estate to join the Third, securing his place as a leader of the Revolution. Despite the fact they were both Freemasons, Lafayette and Louis Philippe were far from close. Louis Philippe became known as *Louis Egalite* and medallions were minted with Louis' image showing the title *Pere du Peuple* (father of the people). He became an obvious choice to replace the King, but overall his position was weak. The King's attempt to escape in June 1791 changed the position for constitutional monarchists like Lafayette, and Louis Philippe voted 'yes' to execute Louis XVI, perhaps in an effort to distance himself from the King and to save his own life. The Reign of Terror was about to descend on France, and Louis Philippe became the centre of suspicion due to a plot involving his son, an officer in the army, who was embroiled in a plan to march on Paris and overthrow the revolutionary government. Instigated in the plot, Louis Philippe was arrested and was guillotined in November 1793.

The Marquis de Lafayette

Lafayette had been involved in the American Revolution and subsequently embraced the French Revolution, supporting liberal reforms but also aware of the need of constitutional monarchy. He was elected vice-president of the National Assembly and elected as head of the Paris Militia (later known as the National Guard) after pacifying the mob who had stormed the Bastille on the 14th July 1789. Lafayette took a direct interest in the new National Constituent Assembly and supported religious tolerance, freedom of the press and the gradual emancipation of slaves, his passion for the reforms being shown in his promotion of the *Declaration of the Rights of Man and of the Citizen* which was adopted by the National Constituent Assembly in August 1789.

Lafayette's devotion to reform and the Revolution did not stop him from gaining critics, one passionate critic being Freemason Jean-Paul Marat. As a nobleman and a monarchist, Lafayette was open to criticism and his actions when commanding the National Guard to open fire on a mob in Paris in July 1791 escalated heated feelings towards Lafayette. He was declared a traitor by the Assembly in August 1792 after rumours of him about to march on Paris to overthrow the revolutionary government. Lafayette, who had been in command of armed forces in preparation to attack Austria, took refuge in Liege where he was subsequently imprisoned for five years, languishing in various Prussian and Austrian prisons, despite the intervention of the United States for his release. His release was finally secured by the French Directory in 1797 but Napoleon wouldn't allow him to return to France until 1799. His wife died in 1807 due to illness brought on by years of imprisonment during the Terror and later with her husband in Austria. He always remained a liberal and supporter of the rights of man despite his hardships.

Jean-Paul Marat

Marat was a physician who had visited England in the early 1770s, and it was during this visit that he was made a Freemason in London, with a Grand Lodge certificate of his membership being issued on the 15th of July, 1774. He held staunch liberal views and wrote the ground-breaking *Chains of Slavery*, which was published in Newcastle in 1774. He returned to France, working as a physician until embracing the spirit of Revolution. On the eve of the Revolution he wanted to influence the progression of the Third Estate, publishing pamphlets and newspapers, one of which was called *The Friend of the People*, in which he constantly criticised people in power and was nearly arrested for his belligerent campaign against fellow Freemason Lafayette. His views became more embittered, Marat attacking the powerful and criticising the National Constituent Assembly, so much so he had to go into hiding in the cellars and catacombs of Paris, which aggravated a skin disease.

Marat's political career reveals the bitterness and blood thirstiness which resulted in the Reign of Terror. After the Revolutionary Paris Commune had started an insurrection on the 10th of August 1792, the Legislative Assembly which had been formed the previous year in support of the constitutional monarchy, collapsed and Louis XVI was imprisoned. The Girondins were liberal republicans who had dominated the Legislative Assembly and had included such leading free thinkers as Thomas Paine. However, their cautious stance on the execution of the King sealed their fate as 'royalists' and their downfall ensued. The radical Jacobins took control and a list of opponents against the revolution was drawn up. Marat came out of hiding and was elected to the National Convention, celebrating the new Republic by ceasing the publication of his newspapers. He still bitterly attacked opponents of radical republicanism, especially the Girondin faction, his fierce propaganda being used by radicals such as Robespierre. As a result of this the Girondins collapsed in June 1793, and Marat, who had outlived his usefulness, began to be distanced from the government. He was assassinated by the Girondin Charlotte Corday the following month who stabbed him to death while he was lying in his bath. She was incensed by the execution of Louis XVI. Marat's death led to reprisals, with thousands of royalists and Girondins being executed by the Guillotine.

These three Freemasons all had a leading role in the development of the Revolution, though they failed to work together and took different sides as the Revolution developed. Only Lafayette survived to see the Restoration and the end of Napoleon, but he also suffered sacrifices for his liberal views. Marat seems to have been overwhelmed with bitterness, attacking Lafayette for being a monarchist and being a member of the nobility. Louis Philippe, the old Grand Master, seems to have been forever tainted with a desire to gain the throne for himself, voting to execute the king and even condemning his own son when the plot was discovered to march on Paris. Because of their involvement in the French Revolution, Freemasonry has become forever linked with Revolutionary ideals, with many modern writers such as Jasper Ridley suggesting deeper connections that the Freemasons in France were behind the Revolution itself. The differences behind these three Masonic figures suggests otherwise, it reflects the complexity of the Revolution and how different political ideas conflicted with personal ideals.

Freemasonry and the Revolution in Latin America

This article was first published in *The Square* in 2016, and followed an article that I co-wrote on the nineteenth century Brazilian revolutionary leader and Freemason Pedro de Alcântara, which appeared in the same magazine previously. It followed similar themes of how Freemasons played a role in revolutions during this period and the style of this piece reflected my previous article on the Freemasonry and the French Revolution; straight to the point and, at the request of the editor, no footnotes.

There were a number of Freemasons involved in the American War of Independence and the French Revolution; prominent men such as , Benjamin Franklin, Lafayette, and Jean Paul Marat. The revolution that emerged in Latin America also involved a number of leading men who were Freemasons or were connected to Freemasonry; revolutionaries such as Simón Bolívar, José de San Martín, Bernardo O'Higgins and Francisco de Miranda. The complicated nexus that interlinks these men and their ideals certainly intertwines with the growth of the Enlightenment of the period and indeed with Freemasonry, as is the shadowy links to Britain that some of these men had at the time.

Francisco de Miranda

Francisco de Miranda was a military commander, revolutionary and Freemason. He was a born in Venezuela in 1750, and after leaving for Spain, he paid for a commission in the Spanish army, and fought in a number of campaigns. He became involved in the American War of Independence and the French Revolution, and met such luminaries of the Enlightenment as George Washington, Thomas Paine and Lafayette, before leading expeditions to invade Venezuela in an attempt to overthrow the Spanish Royalist government. Miranda had developed the idea of an independent Latin America that stretched from the Mississippi River in the north to Cape Horn in the south, and he was to become a figurehead in the quest for revolution in the Spanish American Colonies. In 1806, Miranda managed to obtain informal British help for his expedition, though it ended in failure, Miranda escaping to the British Caribbean, before making his way to Britain, where he endeavoured to gain further support.

A year earlier, he had sought assistance from Thomas Jefferson and James Madison, but they had kept their distance from the scheme. After the failure of the first expedition, another expedition was to be assembled in

1808, headed by none other than erstwhile Freemason Arthur Wellesley – later to be the Duke of Wellington – but Napoleon's invasion of Spain put a stop to the venture. It was to be two years later when, after Napoleon took the Spanish Crown that a junta took control of Caracas, and Miranda was invited to join the new government by Simón Bolívar while he was seeking support on a diplomatic visit to Britain. Miranda was persuaded by his fellow Freemason, but the decision was to be a fatal one; Miranda took the role of leading the Republic's forces, but, by 1812, the Spanish Royalist forces had gained the upper hand, and Miranda, believing the situation to be hopeless, tried to escape on a British ship. He was captured by Bolívar and some fellow revolutionary officers, and was turned over to the Spanish forces, where he was imprisoned, dying in jail in 1816.

José de San Martín

José de San Martín was an Argentinian military commander, revolutionary and Freemason, although his Masonic membership hinges somewhat on his links to the 'Lodge of Rational Knights', otherwise known as the Lautaro Lodge. This lodge was more of a collection of like-minded men who wished to promote the ideals of the Spanish Enlightenment; ideals of liberty and equality under the guise of a Masonic gathering. San Martín had fought in the Peninsular War against France, and was influenced by the ideas of the Spanish Enlightenment while staying in Cadiz, where he may have been introduced to the Lodge of Rational Knights. After 'retiring' from the army and settling in London for a while, he resided at the same house where Freemason Francisco de Miranda had lodged in Grafton Street a number of years before. San Martín then set sail for Argentina in January 1812 on a frigate called *George Canning* – named after the Freemason - with Carlos María de Alvear and Matías Zapiola – two other members of the lodge – and on arriving in Buenos Aires, the three of them formed a new lodge that promoted the ideals of liberty and assisted in spreading the ideas of independence from Spain.

San Martín became colonel of the revolutionary army during a long war with the Royalists; he commanded the Army of the North in Upper Peru, the Army of the Andes which allied San Martín with fellow Freemason Bernardo O'Higgins, who became the leader of Chile, and San Martín became Protector of Peru after declaring its independence in 1821. He met with fellow Freemason and Revolutionary Simón Bolívar at the Guayaquil Conference on the 26th of July, 1822, and there was an intention to join forces and defeat the remnants of the Royalist forces in Peru. However, after the conference, Bolívar and San Martín did not join forces, and San Martín resigned as Protector of Peru, going on to leave South America, living the rest of his life in exile in Europe. He died in 1850, his body eventually being repatriated and finally being laid to rest in Buenos Aires Metropolitan Cathedral in 1880, though, as he was suspected of being a Freemason, his mausoleum was situated in an extended wing of the Cathedral.

Simón Bolívar

Simón Bolívar was a Venezuelan military and political leader, and a Freemason. Bolívar came from an aristocratic *Creole* family, and after his wife died, he ventured to Europe, where he became a Freemason in Cadiz in Spain, his visit shaping his ideas on liberty and on politics; he admired the British politician and Freemason George Canning, and also admired the Romantic poet Lord Byron, who also became involved in revolutionary activities in Greece and had been involved in the quasi-Masonic Carbonari. It was on his return to Venezuela that his political and military ideas could be put to use; after Napoleon had taken the Spanish Crown, Caracas in Venezuela formed a junta in 1810, and Bolívar was among those chosen to travel to London on a diplomatic mission to gain recognition and support. While in London, Bolívar met with Arthur Wellesley and approached the exiled Miranda to become directly involved in the new Venezuelan junta. On arriving back to Venezuela, independence was declared and Miranda, after an introduction by Bolívar, was placed in command of the new Republic's army.

Despite being a Mason, it did not stop Bolívar from arresting fellow Freemason Miranda as a traitor to the Republic in 1812 after suspecting him of fleeing from Spanish Royalist forces, passing him on to the Spanish Royalists who then shipped to Spain to languish in a prison until his death a few years later. Bolívar went on to become a leading commander of the Republican army, being aided by British soldiers fresh from the Napoleonic Wars. He fought tirelessly in Venezuela – helping to restore the Venezuelan Republic twice, both of which he served as President - and in Peru, where he also became President, and a new country was founded in his honour called Bolivia. He was said to have founded a lodge in Peru in 1824 and to have become a Scottish Rite Mason. His vision was to found *Gran Colombia*; a collection of states that included Columbia, Venezuela, Ecuador, Panama, northern Peru, western Guyana and north western Brazil. This vison collapsed after his death in 1830 of tuberculosis, but Bolívar would always be known as *El Libertador* – the Liberator.

Bernardo O'Higgins

Bernardo O'Higgins, as the name suggests, was of both Spanish and Irish descent; he was the illegitimate son of Ambrosio O'Higgins, a Spanish Officer and Adventurer born in Ireland. Bernardo O'Higgins was born in Chile, and though he never met his illustrious father, Ambrosio paid for his education, and he was eventually sent to England to complete this education. It was while he was in London that he met Francisco de Miranda, joining a lodge that had been established by Miranda and becoming introduced to ideas about American independence. Miranda's lodge in London seemed to be similar to the Lautaro Lodge; a collection of men with similar ideas, influenced by the Enlightenment and promoting the vision of an independent Latin America. O'Higgins returned to Chile in 1802 with these ideas, and in 1810, he took a role in acting against the French dominated Spanish government when a junta was formed in Chile. He had some military training and proved himself in battle against the Spanish Royalists, rising to become colonel, but as the republicans were divided with differing ideas on the future of independence, the Spanish Royalists made gains and O'Higgins escaped to Argentina.

It was in Argentina that he met fellow Freemason José de San Martín, who shared a similar political vision to O'Higgins, and together they went to Chile to defeat the Spanish Royalists in 1817, with Chile declaring itself as an independent Republic in 1818. O'Higgins became the Supreme Director of Chile in 1817, a position he held until he was deposed in a coup in 1823. After being deposed, O'Higgins went to Peru where he met with another Freemason Simón Bolívar, and offered support to fight the remaining Royalist forces there. He was to stay exiled in Peru until his death in 1842. His remains were finally returned to Chile in 1869.

For men such as these that sought liberty and equality, Masonic and political visions merged to form a revolutionary idealism. The type of Freemasonry that the Lautaro Lodge practiced and promoted was certainly of a more political flavour; creating an outlet for like-minded men such as Miranda to examine the Enlightenment and to help form a vision for their ideas on a united independent Latin America. These ideas changed South America; creating new countries such as Bolivia, and changing the political structure of Latin America forever.

Antient and Modern

This article was published as a chapter in *The Treasures of English Freemasonry 1717-2017*, the Tercentenary edition by Lewis Masonic. I thought this would be a great piece to end on, as it ties together a number of the themes displayed in some of the articles presented here, with a touch of social history, conflict between Grand Lodges, a touch of rebellion and even a mention of the Wicked Lord Byron. It was published in the book without its footnotes, so I thought I would present it here in its natural state.

The formation of a second Grand Lodge in 1751 caused a major rift in English Freemasonry that would last until 1813; with two Grand Lodges operating on a national scale, both reaching out to the Colonies and each spreading their own particular influence. The later Grand Lodge, somewhat ironically, became known as the Antients and the original or Premier Grand Lodge of 1717 the Moderns. They practiced different methods of administration and had differing attitudes to ritual. An example of the former relates to the way in which the Antients enabled new lodges to purchase the Warrant of a lodge that had ceased operation, thereby retaining the number of the former lodge. The Moderns issued each new lodge with a brand new warrant, this helps explain why there are gaps in lists of lodges and why some lodges have a lower number than older lodges above them in the list. In terms of ritual, the two Grand Lodges both practiced the three degree system, but it was the on-going argument right up to the Union in 1813 concerning the situation of the Royal Arch, which the Antients considered an integral part of Craft Freemasonry whilst the Moderns considered it and indeed worked it as an additional degree.

Laurence Dermott was the leading light the 'Grand Lodge of England according to the Old Institutions', - the Antients, founded in London in 1751 by mainly Irish brethren, who had settled in London, and found it difficult to become members of lodges under the Moderns, which by and large had a membership with a somewhat higher social profile. After Dermott had become Grand Secretary the new Grand Lodge began to attract Masons who amongst other things had become dissatisfied with what they considered to be the modernisation of the Craft. The Antients firmly identified themselves with the older Grand Lodge of York and the Edwin legend. Some alarm was caused amongst the Moderns when the Antients were formally recognised as an official Grand Lodge by both the Scottish and Irish governing bodies. The discontent being expressed by some members of the Craft with their leaders at the time was exemplified in 1764, in an anonymous publication entitled *The Complete Free-mason: or Multa Paucis for Lovers of Secrets*, that attempted to reproach the "Wicked" Lord Byron for the development of the Antients, even though the actual causes of the rebellion dated back to before he became Grand Master.

The Antients soon became extremely influential, its lodges being founded far beyond London, notably in Bristol, which had its own traditional working of the ritual. By 1755, an early Antients lodge could be found in Warrington, the town where Elias Ashmole had become a Mason more than a century before, and Liverpool also boasted a number of early Antients lodges. From ports such as Bristol and Liverpool, the influence of the Antients soon spread overseas to America, other British Colonies and the Continent, mainly due to the Antients granting travelling Warrants for the setting up of lodges within regiments of the British army.

It was Dermott who can be credited with the use of the terms Antient and Modern to distinguish the two English Grand Lodges. Dermott was born in Ireland in 1720 and joined a Dublin Lodge in 1740, which came under the jurisdiction of the Irish Grand Lodge. After moving to England, he joined a Lodge under the jurisdiction of the Premier Grand Lodge in 1748, but switched his allegiance after helping to establish what was to become the Antients in 1751. When *Ahiman Rezon* – the Antient's Book of Constitutions - was first published in 1756, it was almost entirely the work of Dermott who was careful not show any disrespect towards the Modern Freemasonry, though after a number of years, the rift between the two Grand Lodges deepened, and later editions of Dermott's *Constitutions* became increasingly hostile and antagonistic towards the Moderns, who in turn, continually tried to ridicule both Dermott and the Antients.

The Earl of Blessington, who had been the Grand Master of the Irish Grand Lodge in 1738, became the Grand Master of the Antients, Dermott no doubt seeking aristocratic patronage to legitimise the new Grand Lodge. It certainly helped that the first edition of *Ahiman Rezon*, was actually dedicated to Blessington, which must have also helped to cement the relationship between the Antients and the Irish Grand Lodge.

Other Grand Masters of noble birth followed, the most prominent being the third Duke of Atholl, who was installed in 1771, and who in turn helped cement the relationship between the Antients and the Grand Lodge of Scotland; Atholl becoming the Grand Master of the Grand Lodge of Scotland in 1772. His son the fourth Duke of Atholl was installed as Grand

Master in 1775 following the death of the third Duke the previous year. The fourth Duke took office again in 1792, following the death of the Earl of Antrim, and then served as Grand Master, until December 1813, when he stood down in favour of Prince Edward, the Duke of Kent, and thus paved the way for the union between the Antients and the Moderns.

Whilst at local level members there are examples of members interacting and visiting each other's lodges; there were undoubtedly differences between the two different Grand Lodges, particularly amongst the leaders of both Grand Lodges. There is also ample evidence of sustained competition and animosity between the two rival Grand Lodges. Masons from either side who decided to change their allegiance from one to the other, had to swear allegiance and be *"remade"* or *"healed"*, to accord with the ritual of the receiving body. It seems that the *"remaking ceremony"* was even required for members of the Grand Lodge of Scotland wishing to join an English lodge, as occurred in 1774 when two Scottish Masons joined an Antients' lodge. Needless to say there was a fee involved, in September 1785, the sum of one guinea had to be paid for a Modern Mason to be *"re-made"* to become an Antient Mason.

The movement of members between the Modern and Antients continued until the unification in 1813. Thomas Harper, a silversmith and maker of Masonic jewels, was appointed Deputy Grand Master and became a leading figure in the negotiations that reunited the two Grand Lodges. Harper was a member of both the Moderns and the Antients, but was expelled and then reinstated by the Moderns during the course of the proceedings. William Preston, author of *Illustrations of Freemasonry*, had been a member of a lodge under the Antients, switched allegiance to the Moderns, then threw in his lot with the Grand Lodge of All England at York, to assist in the foundation of a new Grand Lodge – the Grand Lodge of All England south of the River Trent, eventually returning to the Moderns.

As time went by local decisions were being made on the matter of *"remaking"*. For example, in the Warrington based Moderns Lodge of Lights, it was agreed in 1803 that if a Brother from an Antient lodge was to be re-admitted, he should be charged the sum of £1 11s 6d, whereas a Brother re-admitted from another Modern lodge should only pay £1 1s.

Some local lodges seemed to hedge their bets, such as the Royal Gloucester Lodge No. 130, in Southampton, which actually held two Warrants - one from the Moderns and one from the Antients. On a number of occasions the members of the lodge transferred their allegiance from one side to the other, never quite being able to decide with which Grand Lodge to stick. Antient lodges, such as No. 86, transacted lodge business in decidedly Modern manner, whilst in Modern lodges, such as the Lodge of Relief, No. 42, in Bury, the terminology used was that of the Antients, as in 1792, when the lodge raised *"Master Masons Ancient"*. Other lodges, such as the Union Lodge, founded in York in 1777, was able to bring together both Antient and Modern Masons in perfect harmony, well before the official Union of 1813.

Instances can be found of rivalry at local level between the Antients and the Moderns. In Chester for example, five months after an Antients lodge had been constituted at the Star Inn in 1766, it found itself usurped by a Modern lodge. An Antient lodge founded at the Bear's Paw in Frodsham near Chester in 1770, had lapsed by 1794. In the second half of the eighteenth century Lodges owing allegiance to the Antients were founded in towns on the fringes of Cheshire: in places like Macclesfield, which had three, and Stockport, which had five, all operating, well away from the Modern stronghold of Chester.

The Antients Grand Lodge was very adaptable in the way it dealt with lodge Warrants, much in the same manner as that adopted by the Grand Lodge of Ireland. To all intents and purposes warrants were considered as transferable. This policy was extremely useful as it meant that new lodges did not have to be consecrated or constituted with all the attendant expense, but could easily be established in other areas simply by transferring an existing warrant from elsewhere. An example is that of the Lodge of St. John, founded in 1765 in Mottram, Longendale in Cheshire. The lodge seemed to have floundered and the Warrant was transferred to Saddleworth in Yorkshire in 1775, with the lodge meeting there until 1784. The Warrant then seemed to have been kept in the possession of one of its old members who took it with him when he moved to Stockport and, after getting it endorsed in London, started the lodge afresh in 1806.

This transfer and re-use of lodge Warrants was very popular. In Liverpool the Antients Lodge No. 25 appeared in 1755, disappeared in the 1760s, only to resurface as an entirely new lodge in Liverpool in 1786. Warrants could also be quickly transferred to other parts of the country, such as the Warrant of Lodge No. 189, an Antients lodge founded in Macclesfield in 1774 that, after being disbanding in 1801, was reissued to the All Saints Lodge in Northumberland the following year.

Warrants bearing an older number were much sought after by members of the Antients. It seems then, as now, that the older the number of the lodge, the more prestige it seems to carry within the Masonic fraternity. At the Union Lodges on both sides had their own numbers and to resolve the situation lots were cast and won by the Antients. As a consequence Grand Master's Lodge of the Antients became No. 1 on the roll of UGLE, whilst the older Modern's Lodge of Antiquity became No. 2 – something that still rankles today. Lodge numbers were then allocated alternately in order of seniority, which helps explains why most of the early former Antients lodges have odd numbers and those of the Moderns even ones. It was only natural that when lodges were renumbered after the Union, and indeed on two subsequent occasions in later years that many lodges, both Antient and Modern, became upset.

Many of the early Antient lodges were short lived and there are no complete surviving records, but the minutes of one lodge in particular, the Lodge of Benevolence, founded in Stockport in 1759, survived. The lodge, which seemed to operate in a similar fashion to a contemporary Modern lodge, got entwined in a financial dispute and surrendered its Antients Warrant, defecting to the Moderns in 1789. The original Warrant of the Lodge of Benevolence was transferred to an Antient lodge in Birmingham in 1811.

In Warrington, an Antient lodge was founded in 1755, which met at The Cock, in Bridge Street but, again, the lodge was short lived, lapsing just over a year later leaving no records. In 1765, the Modern Lodge of Lights was founded and was to dominate Freemasonry in Warrington. The situation was reversed in Liverpool, where during the closing years of the eighteenth century, there were seven Antient lodges while the Moderns could only muster four.

The formation of independent rebel Grand Lodges became almost fashionable during the late eighteenth century. The reasons were manifold, and would have included such things as personal ambition, disputes, or even the desire to work a particular version of the ritual. In 1762, the Antient Grand Lodge dismissed a certain David Fisher who was the Grand Warden elect, after it came to light that he had attempted to form his own Grand Lodge, and had offered to register fellow brethren for 6d each. Ten years earlier, Thomas Phealon and Dr John Macky, two brethren under the Antient Grand Lodge, had also conspired in a somewhat bizarre and maverick fashion, to initiate men into Freemasonry for the price of a leg of mutton. Macky had also initiated Brethren into the Royal Arch, without having any knowledge whatsoever of Royal Arch Masonry, making up the ceremony and instructing that through his teachings of a mysterious Masonic Art, an initiate could become invisible. As a result of these ashamedly blasphemous activities, Dermott expelled Phealon and Macky and ordered that the two men should never be admitted to an Antient lodge ever again.

Another maverick who tried to create a rebel Masonic lodge was Sir Francis Columbine Daniel. He was a doctor, and was first made a Freemason in Lodge No. 3, under the Antients, but he later joined the Royal Naval Lodge that came under the Modern Grand Lodge. Daniel was Master of the Royal Naval Lodge from when he joined in 1791 until 1808, and as a result of issuing certificates on his own authority as Master of the Royal Naval Lodge of Independence; he was dismissed by the Antients in 1801. By 1810, the Moderns also moved against Daniel because of his desire to claim independence for the Royal Naval Lodge. He had initiated almost a thousand men of naval extraction and, due to the large and rapid expansion of the lodge, Daniel seemed to have thought that it was large enough to become independent from the Moderns. Daniel had complained to the Moderns in 1801 about maverick Masons who had been *"encouraging irregular meetings and infringing on the privilege of the Ancient Grand Lodge Of All England assembling under the authority of H.R.H. the Prince of Wales"*.

The Moderns were also strict when dealing with lodges on issues of conformity, especially with certain lodges that wanted to express their individuality. An example of was that of the Country Stewards Lodge, which in 1795, petitioned Grand Lodge to wear aprons trimmed with green to mirror the privilege of Grand Stewards wearing red aprons. The Country Stewards Lodge was composed of Masons who served the Office of Stewards at the country feast of the Grand Lodge. The members of the Lodge had already been given permission to wear a green collar and a distinctive jewel. The request was originally granted and then rescinded causing considerable acrimony to the extent that the last Country Feast took place in 1796, and the Lodge closed in 1802.

Reconciliation

Laurence Dermott, who had twice served as Deputy Grand Master, was fiercely loyal to the cause of the Antients and greatly opposed to any form of unification with the Moderns Grand Lodge. It was not until after he finally retired from the post in 1787 and his death in 1791 that the process of reconciliation between the two Grand Lodges slowly began. As early as 1794, the Duke of Kent, who would eventually become Grand Master of the Antients in responding to a letter signed by the Deputy Grand Masters of both the Antients and the Moderns that suggested a reconciliation:

> *"You may trust that my utmost efforts shall be exerted, that the much-wished-for Union of the whole Fraternity of Masons may be effected."*

Notes

[1] *Minutes of the Royal Lodge of Faith and Friendship, no.270*, Berkeley, Gloucestershire. Not listed.

[2] For a discussion of Joseph Banks' as a Freemason and as President of the Royal Society, see David Harrison, *The Transformation of Freemasonry*, (Bury St. Edmunds: Arima, 2010), pp.24-25.

[3] For a discussion of Erasmus Darwin as a Freemason and a member of the Lunar Society, see David Harrison, *The Genesis of Freemasonry*, (Hersham: Lewis Masonic, 2009), p.50 and p.82.

[4] Jenner's Masonic career was discussed in Harrison, *Genesis of Freemasonry*, p.125 and p.149.

[5] Ibid.

[6] Quotation taken from transcribed letters from Jenner to his friend the Rev. Thomas Pruen in R.B. Fisher Edward Jenner 1749-1823, (London: Andre Deutsch Ltd., 1991), pp.150-1.

[7] For a discussion on the life of Brant see Harrison, *Transformation of Freemasonry*, p.186 and p.187.

[8] See William E. Palmer, *Memoir of the Distinguished Mohawk Indian Chief, Sachem and Warrior, Capt. Joseph Brant, compiled from the most reliable and authentic records. Including a brief history of the principle events of his life, with an appendix and portrait*, (Brantford, Ontario: C.E. Stewart, 1872). This *memoir* discusses Brant's military campaigns during the American War of Independence and also outlines his Masonic membership.

[9] For an analysis of Raffles' Masonic membership see Harrison, *The Transformation of Freemasonry*, pp.110-111 and pp.189-190. See also Sir Thomas Stamford Raffles, Statement of the Services of Sir Stamford Raffles, (London: Cox and Baylie, Great Queen Street, 1824).

[10] Ibid., pp.97-119. Here I examine the Liverpool Masonic scene during the latter eighteenth and early nineteenth centuries and how local Freemasons played an essential role in the trans-Atlantic slave trade.

[11] Ibid., p.37 and p.101. See also P. Jupp, (ed.), *The Letter-Journal of George Canning, 1793-1795*, Royal Historical Society, Camden Fourth Series, Volume 41, (London, 1991), p.202. According to Thomas Fenn, in his *The Prince of Wales's Lodge No.259: list of members from the time of its constitution*, (London: Jarrold & Sons Ltd., Revised ed., 1938), p.33, Canning joined the Prince of Wales Lodge No.259 from Somerset House Lodge on 13th April 1810, though in A.W. Oxford, *No.4 an introduction to the History of the Royal Somerset House and Inverness Lodge*, (London: Bernard Quaritch Ltd, 1928), p.189, it is stated that Canning was initiated and passed in No.4 Lodge on 30th April 1810, although he was proposed on 12th February 1810.

[12] Many thanks to Diane Clements, former Director of library and museum of the UGLE for supplying me with the records of Raffles' Masonic membership.

[13] Anon., *Jachin and Boaz; or, an authentic key to the door of Freemasonry*, (London, 1812), p.11.

[14] See John Day, *Memoir of the Lady Mason*, (Cork, 1996), pp.4-8.

[15] Ibid.

[16] Ibid., pp.8-10.

[17] Ibid., pp.12-15.

[18] See David Harrison, 'Thomas De Quincey: The Opium Eater and the Masonic Text', *AQC*, Vol. 129, (2016), pp.276-281. See also H.J. Jackson, "Swedenborg's *Meaning* is the truth' Coleridge, Tulk, and Swedenborg', *In Search of the Absolute: Essays on Swedenborg and Literature* (Swedenborg Society, 2004). For the influence of Swedenborg on Blake see Peter Ackroyd, *Blake*, (London: QPD, 1995), pp.101-104. Ackroyd discusses how Blake eventually turned against Swedenborg.

[19] Harrison, *Genesis of Freemasonry*, p.97. See also Ackroyd, *Blake*, p.185-187.

[20] Polidori was a member of the Norwich based Union Lodge No. 52, Initiated on the 31st March 1818, Passed on the 28th April 1818 and Raised on the 1st June 1818.

[21] See John William Polidori, *The Vampyre*, (London: Sherwood, Neely and Jones, 1819). See also Peter L. Thorslev, *The Byronic Hero: Types and Prototypes*, (Minneapolis: University of Minnesota Press, 1962).

[22] George Gordon Byron, *Childe Harold's Pilgrimage*, (London: Charles Griffin & Co., 1866), p.54.

[23] *The Trial of William Lord Byron For The Murder of William Chaworth Esq; Before The House of Peers in Westminster Hall, in Full Parliament. London, 1765.* Newstead Abbey Archives, reference NA1051.

[24] See H.J. Whymper 'Lord Byron G.M.', *AQC*, Vol.VI, (1893), pp.17-20.

[25] Ibid., p.17.

[26] Ibid., p.20.

[27] Leslie A. Marchand, (ed.), *Don Juan by Lord Byron*, Canto XIII, Stanza XXIV, (Boston: Houghton Mifflin Company, 1958), p.361.

[28] Ibid, Canto XIV, Stanza XXII, p.385.

[29] See R. Landsdown, 'Byron and the Carbonari', *History Today*, (May, 1991).

[30] See Leslie A. Marchand, (ed.), *Byron's Letters and Journals, Vol. VIII, 'Born for Opposition', 1821*, (Cambridge MA: Harvard University Press, 1978).

[31] See John Belton, 'Revolutionary and Socialist Fraternalism 1848-1870: London to the Italian Risorgimento', *AQC*, Vol.123, (2010), pp.231-253, in which Belton outlines Garibaldi's Masonic career as Grand Hierophant of the Sovereign Sanctuary of Memphis-Misraïm between the years 1881-1882.

[32] See Harrison, *Genesis of Freemasonry*, pp.143-7.

[33] See Margaret Jacob, *The Radical Enlightenment: Pantheists, Freemasons and Republicans*, (London: George Allen & Unwin, 1981).

[34] James Anderson, *Constitutions of the Ancient & Honourable Fraternity of Free & Accepted Masons*, (London: G. Kearsly, 1769), p.203-5.

[35] See G. Treasure, 'Cowper, William, first earl of Cowper, (1665-1723)', *DNB*, 2004.

[36] Anderson, *Constitutions*, (London: 1769), p.203-5. Also see A. Whitaker, *History of No.4 The Royal Somerset House and Inverness Lodge*, (London: Bernard Quaritch Ltd., 1928), p.12.

[37] M. Blackett-Ord, *Hell-Fire Duke: The Life of the Duke of Wharton*, (Berkshire: The Kensall Press, 1982), pp.199-200. Also see Whitaker, *History of No.4 The Royal Somerset House and Inverness Lodge*, p.9.

[38] See J. Kelly, 'Parsons, Lawrence, second earl of Rosse, (1758-1841)', *DNB*, 2004. The third earl of Rosse, William Parsons, was the celebrated astronomer.

[39] See David Stevenson, The Beggar's Benison: Sex Clubs of Enlightenment Scotland and Their Rituals, (East Linton: Tuckwell Press, 2001).

[40] George Rudé, *Wilkes and Liberty*, (Oxford: Oxford University Press, 1972), p.19.

[41] W.J. Chetwode Crawley, 'Mock Masonry in the Eighteenth Century', *AQC*, Vol.XVIII, (1905), pp.128-46.

[42] See Geoffrey Ashe, *The Hell Fire Clubs*, (Stroud: Sutton Publishing, 2000).

[43] See J. Stonehouse, ''The Excavations of Edge Hill, with a Brief Notice of the Late Joseph Williamson', in *The Transactions of the Historic Society of Lancashire and Cheshire*, Volume 68, (1917).

[44] The Joseph Williamson Society is based at the Williamson Tunnels Heritage Centre, on Smithdown Lane, Liverpool. More information can be found on their website: www.williamsontunnels.co.uk [accessed on the 30th of December, 2012]

[45] For information on the Friends of Williamson's Tunnels, see www.williamsontunnels.com [accessed 30th of December, 2012]

[46] See Harrison, *Genesis of Freemasonry*, pp.139-141.

[47] For the history of the Robert Burns Lodge No. 97 and the Malheur Cave, see http://www.burnslodge.org/malheur.html [accessed on the 30th of December, 2012]

[48] K. Arrington, 'Highest Hills or Lowest Vales', www.masonicworld.com [accessed on the 30th of December, 2012]

[49] Many thanks to David Cook for his information on Australian Freemasonry. David Cook was a member of Barron Barnett Lodge of Research No. 146, United Grand Lodge of Queensland, at the time of writing.

[50] See David Harrison, *Liverpool Masonic Rebellion and the Wigan Grand Lodge*.

[51] See Harrison, *Transformation of Freemasonry*, pp.19-36.

[52] P.J. Davey, *Rainford Clay Pipe Industry*, (Oxford: B.A.R., 1982), pp.179-183.

[53] *Minutes of the Lodge of Lights, no.148, 29th of October, 1810*, Warrington Masonic Hall. Not listed.

[54] *Minutes of the Royal Lodge of Faith and Friendship, no.270*, Berkeley, Gloucestershire. Not listed.

[55] Erasmus Darwin joined the St. David's Lodge, No. 36, in Edinburgh in 1754. He was also a member of the renowned Canongate Kilwinning Lodge No. 2.

[56] M. Roberts, *Gothic Immortals*, (London: Routledge, 1990), pp.101-3. Also see D. King-Hele, *Erasmus Darwin and the Romantic Poets*, (London: Macmillan, 1986).

[57] James Watt is discussed as being a member of Somerset House Lodge, see <http://www.mqmagazine.co.uk/issue-17/p-39.php> accessed 23rd of December, 2013. In an alphabetical list of Fellows of the Royal Society who were Freemasons compiled by Bruce Hogg and assisted by Diane Clements (2012), Watt is said to be a member of a Scottish Lodge.

[58] See V. Greenwald, 'Researching the Decoration on a Greatbatch Teapot', in *The American Wedgwoodian*, December 1979, (The Potteries Museum, Stoke-on-Trent).

[59] Joseph Priestley, *Memoirs of Joseph Priestley*, (Allenson, 1904), p.11.

[60] P. O'Brien, *Warrington Academy 1757-86, Its Predecessors & Successors,* (Wigan: Owl Books, 1989), p.21.

[61] See Joseph Priestley, *The History and Present State of Electricity*, (London: Printed for J. Dodsley, J. Johnson and T. Cadell, 1767).

[62] *List of Members of the Lodge of Lights no.148, Warrington, 27th of December, 1766.* Warrington Masonic Hall. Not listed.

[63] A.F.A., Woodford, *Kennings Cyclopaedia of Freemasonry*, (London: Kenning, 1878), p.228.

[64] Ibid.

[65] *List of Members of the Lodge of Lights no.148, Warrington, 28th of July, 1766.* Warrington Masonic Hall. Not listed.

[66] Ibid.

[67] The Castle Lodge No. 122 in Eagle, Colorado, hosts the outdoor lodge event annually with permission of the Colorado Grand Lodge AF&AM. It is put on at Bro. Larry Trotter's TNT Ranch outside of Gypsum Colorado named 'COAZ'.

[68] For the history of the Mullan Pass Historic Lodge No. 1862 which presently meets on the historic site, see http://www.helenamasons.org/MullanPass05.htm [accessed on the 30th of December, 2012]

[69] For the history of the Robert Burns Lodge No. 97 and the Malheur Cave, see http://www.burnslodge.org/malheur.html [accessed on the 30th of December, 2012]

[70] K. Arrington, 'Highest Hills or Lowest Vales', www.masonicworld.com [accessed on the 30th of December, 2012]

[71] Richard Carlile, *The Manual of Freemasonry*, (London: William Reeves, 1912), p.217

[72] Ibid., p.256.

[73] Plato's *Allegory of the Cave* certainly has a theme that resounds in the initiatory experience of Freemasonry. In Plato's *Allegory*, prisoners are shackled in a deep cave within the earth, their reality and thoughts are limited, as all they can see are shadows that are cast on the wall that they face, from objects in front of a fire that is situated behind them. They have no understanding of the world outside, their only reality are the shadows. A prisoner escapes the cave and is exposed to the daylight outside, recognising his previously enslaved state and that his former view of reality was wrong. The first degree reflects this philosophy as the candidate enters the lodge room blindfolded and is later exposed to the light when he becomes a Freemason, starting his new life on a pathway to Masonic enlightenment.

[74] See Harrison, *The Liverpool Masonic Rebellion and the Wigan Grand Lodge*, p.59. In England, Pseudo Masonic clubs, such as the Hell Fire Club, also known as the Monks of Medmenham, certainly met in caves on the estate of Sir Francis Dashwood in West Wycombe during the mid-eighteenth century, and it has been suggested that the cave-like tunnels of Joseph Williamson in Liverpool, constructed in the early nineteenth century, were used as a meeting place of some sorts, but there is no evidence for Masonic meetings in caves in England. See also Harrison, *Genesis of Freemasonry*, pp.139-141. There have been religious gatherings held outside in England, such as the Primitive Methodist meetings of the early nineteenth century held at Mow Cop, the rugged outcrop that straddles the border of Cheshire and Staffordshire, and more recently, the New Age gatherings of Stone Henge during the Summer and Winter Solstice, though in the US, especially in the western States and rural areas of the south, it was common to hold religious meetings outside and conduct baptisms in rivers.

[75] See M.C. Jacob, The Radical Enlightenment: Pantheists, Freemasons and Republicans, (London: George Allen & Unwin, 1981), p.154.

[76] I discussed Thomas Paine's Masonic connections in my first book *The Genesis of Freemasonry*, pp.18-19, and its follow-up *The Transformation of Freemasonry*, p.101 and p.171.

[77] For a more modern examination and transcription of Paine's epic work, see Thomas Paine, *Common Sense*, (London: Pelican Boks, 1976).

[78] See Harrison, *Transformation of Freemasonry*, p.59.

[79] John Dos Passos, Tom Paine, (London: Cassell, 1946), p.22.

[80] See the recent edition Thomas Paine, *De l'origine de la Franc-Maçonnerie*, (Paris: A l'Orient, 2007).

[81] Dos Passos, Tom Paine, p.7.

[82] Ibid., p.43. Paine was associated with Elihu Palmer's Theistical Society, which was also referred

to as the Columbian Illuminati, which was based in New York. See David Harrison, *Rediscovered Rituals of English Freemasonry*, (Hersham: Lewis Masonic, 2020).

[83] See Harrison, *Liverpool Masonic Rebellion and the Wigan Grand Lodge*, p.57.

[84] Norman Rogers, 'The Grand Lodge of Wigan', *AQC*, Vol. LXI, pp.193-5.

[85] See the Presbyterian Church Records, High Street, Stockport, 5th of February 1792, (RG4, 1800, 419).

[86] Harrison, *Liverpool Masonic Rebellion and the Wigan Grand Lodge*, p.58.

[87] See the 1841 Census for Ashton-under-Lyne; John Glover, Inn Keeper, and the 1851 Census for Ashton-under-Lyne; John Glover, Publican and Inn Keeper.

[88] See Harrison, *Transformation of Freemasonry*, pp.11-14.

[89] Ibid.

[90] See David Harrison and John Belton, 'Society in Flux', in *Researching British Freemasonry 1717-2017: JCRFF*, Vol. 3, (Sheffield: University of Sheffield, 2010), pp.71-99.

[91] *List of Members of the Lodge of Lights no.148, Warrington, 28th of July, 1766*. Warrington Masonic Hall. Not listed.

[92] See David Harrison, 'Freemasonry, Industry and Charity: The Local Community and the Working Man', *The Journal of the Institute of Volunteering Research*, Volume 5, Number 1, (2002), pp.33-45.

[93] Ibid.

[94] For a complete analysis of Richard Carlile and his *Manual of Freemasonry*, see the forthcoming publication by David Harrison, *Rediscovered Rituals of English Freemasonry*, (Hersham: Lewis Masonic, 2020).

[95] For information on the Merchants Lodge in Liverpool, see Harrison, *Transformation of Freemasonry*, pp.97-119, and also Harrison, *Liverpool Masonic Rebellion and the Wigan Grand Lodge*.

[96] Ibid.

Bibliography

Primary Source Material

List of Members of the Lodge of Lights No.148, Warrington, 1765-1981, Warrington Masonic Hall. Not listed.

List of the Members of Lodge No. 428 (Merchants Lodge), 1789. Liverpool Masonic Hall, Hope Street, Liverpool. Not listed.

List of Members & Minutes of the Lodge of Friendship, No.277, Oldham Masonic Hall, 1789-1900. Not listed.

Minutes from the Amicable Club, 1788-1803, Warrington Library, reference MS13.

Minutes from the Eagle & Child Club, 1781-1785, Warrington Library, reference MS14.

The Minute Books for the Mechanics Institute, 1838-1855, Warrington Library, reference MS235.

Minutes of the Lodge of Lights No.148, 1850-1900, Warrington Masonic Hall. Not listed.

Minutes of the Ancient Union Lodge no. 203, 1795-1835, Garston Masonic Hall, Liverpool. Not listed.

Minutes of the Lodge of Harmony no. 220, 1822-1835, Garston Masonic Hall, Liverpool. Not listed.

Minutes of the Royal Lodge of Faith and Friendship, no.270, Berkeley, Gloucestershire. Not listed.

Minutes of the Toxteth Lodge No. 1356, Liverpool, 1871-2009. Held by the Lodge. Not listed.

Reminiscences of an Unrecognized Lodge, namely Old Sincerity Lodge No. 486 by James Miller. Many thanks to the Rev. Neville Cryer who supplied the memoirs of James Miller. Not listed.

Published Source Material

Anderson, James, *The Constitutions of The Free-Masons,* (London: Senex, 1723).

Anderson, James, *Constitutions of the Ancient & Honourable Fraternity of Free & Accepted Masons,* (London: G. Kearsly, 1769).

Anon., *The Trial of William Lord Byron For The Murder of William Chaworth Esq; Before The House of Peers in Westminster Hall, in Full Parliament. London, 1765.* Newstead Abbey Archives, reference NA1051.

Anon., *Jachin and Boaz; or, an authentic key to the door of Freemasonry,* (London, 1812).

Anon., *The Life of Captain Joseph Brant with An Account of his Re-interment at Mohawk, 1850, and of the Corner Stone Ceremony in the Erection of the Brant Memorial, 1886,* (Ontario, Brantford: B.H. Rothwell, 1886).

Anon., *Liverpool & Slavery by a Genuine Dicky Sam*, (Newcastle on Tyne: F. Graham, 1969 Edition).

Ashmole, Elias, *Theatrum Chemicum Britannicum*, (London, 1652).

Barbauld, Anna Laetitia, *Poems by Anna Laetitia Barbauld*, (Boston: Wells and Lilly, 1820).

Barbauld, Anna Laetitia, *The Works of Anna Laetitia Barbauld With a Memoir by Lucy Aikin*, (Boston: David Reed, 1826).

Bligh Bond, Frederick, *Central Somerset Gazette Illustrated Guide to Glastonbury*, (Glastonbury: Avalon Press, 1927).

Bligh Bond, Frederick, *The Gate of Remembrance, The story of the psychological experiment which resulted in the discovery of the Edgar Chapel at Glastonbury*, (Kessinger Publishing Co., 1999).

Boswell, James, *Boswell's Life of Johnson*, (London: John Murray, 1847).

Burke, Edmund, 'Reflections on the Revolution in France, and on the proceedings in certain societies in London relative to that event: In a letter intended to have been sent to a gentleman in Paris', in *The Works of The Right Honorable Edmund Burke, Revised Edition, Vol. III*, (Boston: Little, Brown, and Company, 1865).

Carlile, Richard, *The Manual of Freemasonry*, (London: William Reeves, 1912).

Conan Doyle, Arthur, *The History of Spiritualism*, (Teddington: Echo Library, 2006).

Conan Doyle, Arthur, *The Coming of the Fairies*, (Forgotten Books, 2007).

Coustos, John, *The Sufferings of John Coustos for Free-Masonry And For His Refusing to Turn Roman Catholic in the Inquisition at Lisbon*, (London: W. Strahan, 1746).

Craig, R., & Jarvis, R., *Liverpool Registry of Merchant Ships*, Vol. 15, (Manchester: Chatham Society, 1967).

Crow, Hugh, *Memoirs of the late Captain Hugh Crow of Liverpool*, (Liverpool: Longman, Rees, Orme, Brown & Green, and G. & J. Robinson, 1830).

Cunningham, Peter, *Hand-Book of London, past and present*, (London: J. Murray, 1850).

Davies, J. A., (ed.), *The Letters of Goronwy Owen (1723-1769)*, (Cardiff: William Lewis Ltd, 1924).

Desaguliers, J.T., *A Dissertation Concerning the Figure of the Earth*, The Royal Society Library, London, (1724).

Dickens, Charles, Jr, *Dictionary Of London: An Unconventional Handbook*, (London: Charles Dickens and Evans, 1879).

Duncan, Malcolm C., *Duncan's Masonic Ritual and Monitor*, (Forgotten Books, 2008).

Fatout, Paul, *Mark Twain Speaking*, (Iowa: University of Iowa Press, 1978).

Fenn, Thomas, The Prince of Wales's Lodge No. 259: list of members from the time of its constitution, (London: Jarrold & Sons Ltd., Revised ed. 1938).

Forster, George, *A Voyage Round The World, Vol. I & II*, (White, Robson, Elunsley & Rhodes, 1777).

Franklin, Benjamin, *The Autobiography of Benjamin Franklin*, (New York: Courier Dover Publications, 1996).

Gore's Liverpool Trade Directory, 1825, Liverpool Library. Ref: H942.7215.

Gronow, Captain R.H., *Celebrities of London and Paris*, (London: Smith, Elder & Co., 1865).

Gronow, Captain R.H., *Reminiscences of Captain Gronow*, (London: Smith, Elder & Co., 1862).

Hunt, Leigh, *The Poetical Works of Leigh Hunt and edited by his son Thornton Hunt*, (London: George Routledge and Sons, 1860).

Hunt, Leigh, *The Town*, (Oxford: Oxford University Press, 1907).

Idzerda, Stanley J., (ed.), *Lafayette in the Age of the American Revolution: Selected Letters and Papers 1776-1790*, Vol.I, December 7, 1776-March 30, 1778, (New York: Cornell University Press, 1983).

Jupp, P., (ed.), *The Letter-Journal of George Canning, 1793-1795*, Royal Historical Society, Camden Fourth Series, Volume 41, (London, 1991).

Kipling, Rudyard, *Many Inventions*, (Kessinger Publishing Reprint, 2005).

Malthus, Thomas, *An Essay on the Principle of Population as it Affects the Future Improvement of Society*, (London: Printed for J. Johnson, 1798).

Marchand, Leslie A., (ed.), *Don Juan by Lord Byron*, Canto XIII, Stanza XXIV, (Boston: Houghton Mifflin Company, 1958).

Marchand, Leslie A., (ed.), *Byron's Letters and Journals, Vol. VIII, 'Born for Opposition', 1821*, (Cambridge MA: Harvard University Press, 1978).

Moore, Charles W., Grand Secretary of The Grand Lodge of Massachusetts, *The Freemasons' Monthly Magazine*, Vol. XXIII, (Boston: printed by Hugh H. Tuttle, 1864).

Moss, W., *The Liverpool Guide*, (Printed for and sold by Crane and Jones, Castle Street, sold by Vernor and Hood, London, 1796).

Paine, Thomas, *Origin of Free Masonry*, in *The Works of Thomas Paine*, (New York: E. Haskell, 1854).

Paine, Thomas, *Rights of Man: Being An Answer to Mr. Burke's Attack on The French Revolution*, (London: Holyoake and Co., 1856).

Paine, Thomas, *Common Sense*, (London: Pelican Books, 1976).

Paine, Thomas, 'African Slavery in America' (1775), in Micheline Ishay, (ed.), *The human rights reader: major political writings, essays, speeches, and documents from the Bible to the present*, (Routledge, 1997).

Paine, Thomas, *De l'origine de la Franc-Maçonnerie*, (Paris: A l'Orient, 2007).

Palmer, William E., *Memoir of the Distinguished Mohawk Indian Chief, Sachem and Warrior, Capt. Joseph Brant, compiled from the most reliable and authentic records. Including a brief history of the principle events of his life, with an appendix and portrait*, (Brantford, Ontario: C.E. Stewart, 1872).

Pike, Albert, *Morals and Dogma of the Ancient and Accepted Scottish Rite of Freemasonry*, (NuVision Publications LLC, 2007).

Polidori, William John, *The Vampyre*, (London: Sherwood, Neely and Jones, 1819).

Price, Richard, 'Additional Observations on the Nature and Value of Civil Liberty, and the War with America', (1777), in David Oswald Thomas, (ed.), *Political Writings by Richard Price*, (Cambridge: Cambridge University Press, 1991).

Priestley, Joseph, *The History and Present State of Electricity*, (London: Printed for J. Dodsley, J. Johnson and T. Cadell, 1767).

Priestley, Joseph, *Lectures on History and General Policy*, (Dublin: P. Byrne, 1788).

Priestley, Joseph, *The Memoirs of Joseph Priestley*, (Allenson, 1904).

Raffles, Sir Thomas Stamford, *Statement of the Services of Sir Stamford Raffles*, (London: Cox and Baylie, Great Queen Street, 1824).

Raffles, Sophia, *Memoir of the Life and Public Services of Sir Thomas Stamford Raffles FRS*, Vol. 1, (London: James Duncan, 1835).

Stukeley, William, *Stonehenge a temple restor'd to the British Druids*, (W. Innys and R. Manby, 1740).

Viscount Leverhulme by his son, (London: Allen & Unwin Ltd., 1928).

Walesby, F.P., (ed.), *The Works of Samuel Johnson*, (Oxford: Talboys and Wheeler, 1825).

Walsh, Robert, (ed.), *Select Speeches of the Right Honourable George Canning with a Preliminary Biographical Sketch, and an Appendix of Extracts From His Writings and Speeches*, (Philadelphia: Crissy & Markley, 1850).

Warren, Sir Herbert, (ed.), *Poems of Alfred, Lord Tennyson 1830-1865*, (Oxford: Oxford University Press, 1929).

Wilde, Oscar, *The Complete Works*, (London: Magpie, 1993).

Yeats, W.B., 'The Secret Rose' in R.K.R. Thornton, (ed.), *Poetry of the 'Nineties*, (Middlesex: Penguin, 1970).

Secondary Works

Ackroyd, Peter, *Blake*, (London: QPD, 1995)

Armstrong, John, *History of the Lodge of Lights, no. 148,* (Warrington, 1898).

Armstrong, John, *A History of Freemasonry in Cheshire*, (London: Kenning, 1901).

Armstrong, James, *Freemasonry in Warrington from 1646 Onwards*, (Warrington: John Walker, 1935).

Arrowsmith, P., *Stockport - a History*, (Stockport MBC, 1997).

Ashe, Geoffrey, *The Hell Fire Clubs*, (Stroud: Sutton Publishing, 2000).

Barrow, G., *Celtic Bards, Chief's and Kings*, (London: John Murray, 1928).

Barty-King, Hugh, *"Round Table" The Search for Fellowship 1927-1977*, (London: Heinemann, 1977).

Beesley, E.B., *The History of the Wigan Grand Lodge*, (Leeds: Manchester Association for Masonic Research, 1920).

Begemann, Wilhelm, *Vorgeschite und Anfäfnge der Freimaurerei in England* (Berlin: Ernst Siegfried Mittler und Sohn, 1909).

Belton, John, 'Revolutionary and Socialist Fraternalism 1848-1870: London to the Italian Risorgimento', *AQC*, Vol.123, (2010), pp.231-253.

Bennet, A., *A Glance at some old Warrington Societies*, (Warrington: Mackie & Co. Ltd, 1906).

Blackett-Ord, M., *Hell-Fire Duke: The Life of the Duke of Wharton*, (Berkshire: The Kensall Press, 1982).

Blocker, Jack S., Fahey, David M., and Tyrrell, Ian R., *Alcohol and Temperance in Modern History*, (ABC-CLIO Ltd., 2003).

Bullock, S.C., *Revolutionary Brotherhood*, (North Carolina: University of North Carolina Press, 1996).

Calvert, Albert F., 'Where Masons Used to Meet', in the *British Masonic Miscellany*, Compiled by George M. Martin, Vol.20, (Dundee: David Winter and Son, 1936), pp.95-98.

Carter, G.A., *Warrington Hundred*, (Warrington, 1947).

Crowe, A.M., *Warrington, Ancient and Modern*, (Warrington: Beamont Press, 1947).

Davey, P.J., *Rainford Clay Pipe Industry*, (Oxford: B.A.R., 1982).

Davie, Grace, *Religion in Britain Since 1945: Believing Without Belonging*, (Oxford: Wiley-Blackwell, 1994).

Day, John, *Memoir of the Lady Mason*, (Cork, 1996).

Debo, Angie, *The Road to Disappearance, A History of the Creek Indians*, (Oklahoma: The University of Oklahoma Press, 1941).

Dos Passos, John, *Tom Paine*, (London: Cassell, 1946).

Evans, E. J., *The Forging of the Modern State: Early Industrial Britain 1783-1870*, (London: Longman, 1992).

Faulks, Philippa and Cooper, Robert L.D., *The Masonic Magician; The Life and Death of Count Cagliostro and his Egyptian Rite*, (London: Watkins, 2008).

Fort Newton, Joseph, *The Builders*, (London: Unwin Brothers Limited, 1924).

Gee, B., *History of the Lodge of Friendship no.277*, (Oldham, 1989).

Gosden, P.H.J.H., *The Friendly Societies In England 1815-1875*, (Manchester: Manchester University Press, 1961).

Gould, R.F., *The History of Freemasonry, Vol. I-VI*, (London, 1884-7).

Greer, Mary K., *Women of the Golden Dawn; Rebels and Priestesses*, (Rochester, Vermont: Park Street Press, 1995).

Haakonssen, Lisbeth, *Medicine and Morals in the Enlightenment: John Gregory, Thomas Percival and Benjamin Rush*, (Amsterdam: Rodopi, 1997).

Harland-Jacobs, Jessica, *Builders of Empire: Freemasonry and British Imperialism 1717-1927*, (North Carolina: North Carolina Press, 2007).

Harrison, David, *The Genesis of Freemasonry*, (Hersham: Lewis Masonic, 2009).

Harrison, David, *The Liverpool Masonic Rebellion and the Wigan Grand Lodge*, (Bury St. Edmunds: Arima, 2012).

Harrison, David, *Rediscovered Rituals of English Freemasonry*, (Hersham: Lewis Masonic, 2020).

Hewitt, C.R., *Towards My Neighbour: The Social Influence of the Rotary Club Movement in Great Britain and Ireland*, (London: Longmans, 1950).

Hobsbawm, E. J., *Labouring Men*, (London: Weidenfeld and Nicolson, 1986).

Hoffmann, Stefan-Ludwig, *The Politics of Sociability: Freemasonry and German Civil Society, 1840-1918*, Translated by Tom Lampert, (University of Michigan Press, 2007).

Hyneman, Leon, *Freemasonry in England from 1567 to 1813*, (Montana: Kessinger Publishing, 2003).

Jacob, Margaret, *The Radical Enlightenment: Pantheists, Freemasons and Republicans*, (London: George Allen & Unwin, 1981).

Jones, Peter, (ed.), *The French Revolution in Social & Political Perspective*, (London: Arnold, 1996).

Kelly, T., *A History of Adult Education in Great Britain*, (Liverpool: Liverpool University Press, 1970).

Kingsford, P.W., *Engineers, Inventors and Workers*, (London: Edward Arnold, 1973).

Longmate, N., *The Hungry Mills*, (London: Temple Smith, 1978).

Lovett, T., *Adult Education Community Development & The Working Class*, (Department of Adult Ed., University of Nottingham, 1982).

Mackey, Albert Gallatin, *A Lexicon of Freemasonry*, (London, 1869).

Mackey Albert Gallatin, and Haywood, H.L., *Encyclopedia of Freemasonry Part 1*, (Montana: Kessinger, 1946).

Macnab, John, History of The Merchants Lodge, No. 241, Liverpool, 1780-2004, Second Edition, (Liverpool, 2004).

McLachlen, H., *Warrington Academy, Its History and Influence*, (Manchester: The Chetham Society, 1968).

Moran, Maureen, *Victorian Literature and Culture*, (New York: Continuum, 2006).

Nulty, G., *Guardian Country 1853-1978*, (Cheshire County Newspapers Ltd, 1978).

O'Brien, P., *Warrington Academy, 1757-86, Its Predecessors & Successors*, (Owl Books, 1989).

O'Brien, P., *Eyres' Press, 1756-1803, An Embryo University Press*, (Owl Books, 1993).

O'Brien, P., M.D., *Debate Aborted: Burke, Priestley, Paine & The Revolution in France 1789-91*, (Durham: Pentland Press, 1996).

Oxford, A.W., *No. 4 an introduction to the History of the Royal Somerset House and Inverness Lodge*, (London: Bernard Quaritch Ltd., 1928).

Picton, J. A., *Memorials of Liverpool*, Vol. I, (London: Longmans, 1875).

Putnam, R.D., *Bowling Alone: The Collapse and Revival of American Community*, (New York: Simon & Schuster, 2000).

Putnam, R.D., *Democracies in Flux: The Evolution of Social Capital in Contemporary Society*, (New York: Oxford University Press 2002).

Roberts, Allen E., *House Undivided: The Story of Freemasonry and the Civil War*, (Missouri, USA: Missouri Lodge of Research, 1961).

Roberts, M., *Gothic Immortals*, (London: Routledge, 1990).

Rudé, George, *Wilkes and Liberty*, (Oxford: Oxford University Press, 1972).

Rule, J., (ed.), *British Trade Unionism 1750 - 1850: The Formative Years*, (Longman, 1988).

Sandbach, R.S.E., *Priest and Freemason: The Life of George Oliver*, (Northamptonshire: The Aquarian Press, 1988).

Saxelby, C. H., (ed.), *Bolton Survey (County History Reprints)*, (Bolton: SR Publishers, 1971).

Stephens, W.B., *Adult Education And Society In An Industrial Town: Warrington 1800-1900*, (University of Exeter, 1980).

Stevenson, David, The Beggar's Benison: Sex Clubs of Enlightenment Scotland and Their Rituals, (East Linton: Tuckwell Press, 2001).

Surrey Dane, E., *Peter Stubs and the Lancashire Hand Tool Industry*, (John Sherratt and Son Ltd, 1973).

Tait, A., *History of the Oldham Lyceum 1839-1897*, (Oldham: H.C. Lee, 1897).

Thomas, H., *The Slave Trade*, (New York: Simon & Schuster Inc., 1997).

Thompson, E.P., *The Making of the English Working Class*, (Pelican, 1970).

Thorslev, Peter, L., *The Byronic Hero: Types and Prototypes*, (Minneapolis: University of Minnesota Press, 1962).

Turner, W., *The Warrington Academy*, (Warrington: The Guardian Press 1957).

Williams, Gomer, *History of the Privateers and Slave Trade of Liverpool*, (Liverpool: Edward Howell, 1906).

Willey, B., *The Eighteenth Century Background*, (Chatto & Windus, 1946).

Wood, Robert Leslie, *York Lodge No. 236, formerly The Union Lodge, the be-centennial history 1777-1977*, (York, 1977).

Woodford, A.F.A., *Kennings Cyclopaedia of Freemasonry*, (London: Kenning, 1878).

Woods, Herbert, and Armstrong, James, *A Short Historical Note of Freemasonry in Warrington*, (Warrington, 1938).

Journals

Alexander, Jennifer S., 'The Introduction and Use of Masons' Marks in Romanesque Buildings in England', in *Medieval Archaeology*, 51, (2007), pp.63-81.

Ashworth, William J., 'Memory, Efficiency, and Symbolic Analysis: Charles Babbage, John Herschel, and the Industrial Mind', *ISIS*, Vol.87, No.4, USA, (1996), pp.629-653.

Belton, John L., 'Masonic Membership Myths Debunked', in *Heredom*, Vol. 9, (Washington DC: Scottish Rite Research Society, 2001), pp.9-32.

Belton, John L., 'Communication and Research versus Education' – the battle for a master mason's daily advance in Masonic knowledge', *AQC*, Vol. 118, (2006), pp.210-218.

Begemann, W., 'An Attempt to Classify the "Old Charges" of the British Masons', in *AQC*, Vol. 1, (1888), pp.152-167.

Burt, Roger, 'Industrial Relations In The British Non-Ferrous Mining Industry in the Nineteenth Century', in *Labour History Review*, Vol. 71, No. 1, (April 2006), pp.57-79.

Chetwode Crawley, W.J., 'Mock Masonry in the Eighteenth Century', *AQC*, Vol. XVIII, (1905), pp.128-46.

Durr, Andy, 'Chicken and Egg – the Emblem Book and Freemasonry: the Visual and Material Culture of Associated Life', in *AQC*, Vol. 118, (2006), pp.20-36.

Gilbert, R.A., 'The Masonic Career of A.E. Waite', in *AQC*, Vol. 99, (1986).

Gould, R.F., 'English Freemasonry Before the Era of Grand Lodge', in *AQC*, Vol. 1, (1888), pp.67-74.

Greenwald, V., 'Researching the Decoration on a Greatbatch Teapot', in *The American Wedgwoodian*, December 1979, (The Potteries Museum, Stoke-on-Trent).

Halstead, J., and Prescott, A., 'Breaking The Barriers: Masonry, Fraternity And Labour', *Labour History Review*, Vol. 71, No. 1, (April 2006), pp.3-8.

Harrison, David, 'Freemasonry, Industry and Charity: The Local Community and the Working Man'. *The Journal of the Institute of Volunteering Research*, Volume 5, Number 1, (Winter 2002), pp.33-45.

Harrison, David and Belton, John, 'Society in Flux' in *Researching British Freemasonry 1717-2017: The Journal for the Centre of Research into Freemasonry and Fraternalism*, Vol. 3, (Sheffield: University of Sheffield, 2010), pp.71-99.

Harrison, David, 'Thomas De Quincey: The Opium Eater and the Masonic Text', *AQC*, Vol. 129, (2016), pp.276-281.

Harrison, David, 'Sex, Seduction, and Secret Societies: Byron, the Carbonari and Freemasonry', in *Acta Macionica*, Vol.27, (2017), pp.85-95.

Jackson, H.J., "Swedenborg's *Meaning* is the truth' Coleridge, Tulk, and Swedenborg', *In Search of the Absolute: Essays on Swedenborg and Literature* (Swedenborg Society, 2004).

Jupp, P., (ed.), *The Letter-Journal of George Canning, 1793-1795*, Royal Historical Society, Camden Fourth Series, Volume 41, (London, 1991).

Klein, Lawrence, 'The Third Earl of Shaftesbury and the Progress of Politeness', *Eighteenth-Century Studies*, Vol. 18, No. 2, (Winter, 1984-1985), pp.186-214.

Klein, Lawrence E., 'Liberty, Manners, and Politeness in Early Eighteenth-Century England', *The Historical Journal*, Vol. 32, No. 3, (September, 1989), pp.583-605.

Landsdown, R., 'Byron and the Carbonari', *History Today*, (May, 1991).

Mill, John S., 'The Corn Laws', in *The Westminster Review*, Vol. 3, (April 1825).

Money, John, 'The Masonic Moment; Or Ritual, Replica, and Credit: John Wilkes, the Macaroni Parson, and the Making of the Middle-Class Mind', in *The Journal of British Studies*, Vol. 32, No. 4, (October, 1993), pp.358-95.

Porter, George R., 'Free Trade', in *The Edinburgh Review*, Vol. 90, (July 1849).

Putnam, R.D., 'Bowling Alone: America's Declining Social Capital', in *Journal of Democracy*, Volume 6, Number 1, (Baltimore, Maryland, USA: Johns Hopkins University Press, January 1995).

Read, Will, 'The Spurious Lodge and Chapter at Barnsley', in *AQC*, Vol. 90, (1978), pp.1-36.

Sandbach, R.S.E., 'Robert Thomas Crucefix, 1788-1850', in *AQC*, Vol. 102, (1990), pp.134-163.

Seemungal, L.A., 'The Rise of Additional Degrees' in *AQC*, Vol. 84, (1971), pp.307-312.

Spurr, Michael J., 'The Liverpool Rebellion', in *AQC*, Vol. 85, (1972), pp.29-60.

Starr, Martin P., 'Aleister Crowley: Freemason!', in *AQC*, Vol. 108, (1995), pp.150-161.

Stonehouse, J., ''The Excavations of Edge Hill, with a Brief Notice of the Late Joseph Williamson', in *The Transactions of the Historic Society of Lancashire and Cheshire*, Volume 68, (1917).

Warren, Sir Charles, 'On the Orientation of Temples', in *AQC*, Vol. 1, (1888), pp.36-50.

Westcott, W.W., 'The Religion of Freemasonry illuminated by the Kabbalah', in *AQC*, Vol. 1, (1888), pp.55-59.

Woodford, A.F.A., 'Freemasonry and Hermeticisim', in *AQC*, Vol. 1, (1888), pp.28-36.

Whymper, H.J., 'Lord Byron G.M.', *AQC*, Vol.VI, (1893), pp.17-20.

Vatcher, S., 'John Coustos and the Portuguese Inquisition', *AQC*, Vol. 81, (1968), pp.50-51.

Index

Other Titles by David Harrison

The Transformation of Freemasonry
ISBN: 978-1-84549-437-7

The Liverpool Masonic Rebellion and the Wigan Grand Lodge
ISBN: 978-1-84549-561-9

The York Grand Lodge
ISBN: 978-1-84549-629-6

Christopher Rawdon: the lost philanthropiste
ISBN: 978-1-84549-692-0

www.ingramcontent.com/pod-product-compliance
Lightning Source LLC
Chambersburg PA
CBHW050843270326
41930CB00019B/3447